# *Helga Braemer*
# *Ines Scheurmann*

# *Tropical Fish*

## Everything about Freshwater Aquariums and the Selection and Care of Fish

With 42 Color Photographs by Outstanding Animal
Photographers and 78 Drawings by Fritz W. Köhler

*Translated by* Waltraut Riave

## Barron's
### New York / London / Toronto / Sydney

First English language edition published in 1983 by Barron's Educational Series, Inc.
© 1982 by Gräfe and Unzer GmbH, Munich, West Germany.

The title of the German book is *Aquarienfische*.

*All inquiries should be addressed to:*
Barron's Educational Series, Inc.
250 Wireless Boulevard
Hauppauge, New York 11788

*Library of Congress Catalog Card No. 83-9951*
International Standard Book No. 0-8120-2686-1

**Library of Congress Cataloging in Publication Data**
Braemer, Helga, 1928–
    Tropical fish.

    Translation of: Aquarienfische.
    Bibliography: p.
    Includes index.
    Summary: A manual outlining the selection and care of tropical fish and how to set up and maintain an aquarium.
    I. Tropical fish.  2. Aquariums.  [1. Tropical fish.  2. Aquariums]  I. Scheurmann, Ines, 1950–  II. Köhler, Fritz W., ill.  III. Title.
    SF457.B6713  1983      639.3′4      83-9951
    ISBN 0-8120-2686-1

PRINTED IN HONG KONG
789     490     16 15 14 13 12 11 10

**Dr. Helga Braemer**
Born in 1928 in Freiburg/Breisgau, Helga Braemer studied biology in Freiburg, Basel, and Tübingen and took her doctorate in Tübingen in 1955. Her special area of study is the sensory physiology of fishes.

**Ines Scheurmann**
Born in 1950 in Kleba, county of Hersfeld, Ines Scheurmann studied biology in Giessen. Her doctoral dissertation was on the reproductive behavior of Cichlids, and her present field of specialization is fish behavior.

Cover design: Constanze Reithmayr-Frank

Front cover: Angelfish or Scalare *(Pterophyllum scalare)* with spawn.
Inside front cover: Giant Danios *(Danio aequipinnatus [malabaricus])*. The fish in the upper left corner of the photo is a Pearl Danio *(Brachydanio albolineatus)*.
Inside back cover: Densely planted aquarium with various kinds of Characins.
Back cover: (above left) Pink-Tailed Australian Rainbow *(Melanotaenia splendida);* (above right) Guppy *(Poecilia reticulata);* (below left) Kribensis *(Pelvicachromis pulcher)*; (below right) Black-Spotted Corydoras *(Corydoras melanistius)*.

*Photographs*
Hansen:      page 46 (above left)
Kahl:        inside back cover, back cover (below left, below right), pages 17 (above left, middle left, middle right, below right), 18, 35, 36 (above left, middle left, middle right, below left, below right), 46 (above right, middle right, below right), 63 (middle right, below left), 64 (middle left, middle right, below left)
NHPA/Lemoine: page 63 (below right)
Reinhardt:   front cover, inside front cover, back cover (above left, above right), pages 17 (above right, below left), 36 (above right), 45, 46 (middle left, below left), 63 (above left, above right, middle left), 64 (above left, above right, below right)

# Contents

# Preface

A beautifully decorated and well cared for aquarium can be an attractive addition to any home. Looking at the green plants and the brightly colored fish darting among them is stimulating and calming at the same time. No special talents are needed to keep aquarium fish, but some basic knowledge is useful, and this pet owner's guide contains all the necessary information in concise and easily understandable form.

This little book is intended for novice aquarists. It is especially designed to help children who have been given a tank with some fish in it. But we do assume that the children have had some experience in reading books and are able to understand some simple processes in physics and chemistry. Of course, adult family members should stand by during the first months, offering help and advice as needed. Many new aquarium owners soon give up this enjoyable hobby because — in spite of all their well-intentioned care — the fish become ill and die, or algae take over. Our little book is addressed to these hobbyists, too. Here they will find how to take care of an aquarium properly and keep the fish in it healthy.

The first thing an aquarist should think about is the water for the tank. To put it in a nutshell: If the water is right, the fish will do well. That is why the first chapter on choosing a tank is followed immediately by a detailed chapter on how to create and maintain the proper water conditions. Then we tell you about essential equipment and useful accessories. We mention just a few of the many available products to give you an idea of the range of offerings. It is possible to find something to fit just about any kind of home and any size budget. Dealers will be happy to advise you when you choose your aquarium and accessories.

In the remaining chapters, we introduce the occupants of the aquarium — fish, plants, snails — and tell you how to take care of them. We have consciously limited ourselves to fishes and plants for tropical freshwater aquariums because they are easier to look after than cold-water and salt-water fish. And among warm-water fish, we have selected — with a few exceptions — those which get along well with each other and present few problems for a beginner.

It is a good idea for a novice to start out with livebearers such as Guppies and Swordtails. As he gains experience, he can begin to breed fish, keep more demanding species, or set up a special type of aquarium, like the so-called Dutch plant aquarium or a biotope aquarium.

The special section "Understanding Fish" grew out of and reflects our everyday work as biologists. Regarding the behavioral patterns of fish as a kind of language can be a key that opens up many exciting experiences.

The many color photos and drawings in the book convey a sense of how extraordinarily beautiful tropical fish are and how interesting the hobby of keeping fish can be. We would like to take this opportunity to thank the photographers, especially Mr. Reinhard and Mr. Kahl, and the artist Fritz W. Köhler, for their collaboration on this book.

*Helga Braemer*
*Ines Scheurmann*

# The Correct Aquarium

Your first and most important purchase is the tank or aquarium. You also need a heater to maintain tropical water temperatures in the tank, lamps to light it up, and a filter and ventilation system. All this equipment must be suited to the particular needs of the future inhabitants of the aquarium. When you set up an aquarium, you should not be penny-wise. A tank and accessories that are inexpensive but inadequate will prove a source of annoyance for years to come. In this chapter you will find mention of everything you should watch out for to prevent later disappointment.

## What Kind of Tank?

The aquariums that are on the market today are much better and more durable than those that were available twenty years ago.

*Tanks made of glass* come in two types: frame tanks (see drawing on this page) with frames made of anodized aluminum, plastic, or stainless steel, and frameless tanks (see drawing on page 6). Both types are caulked with silicone rubber; they do not rust and can be used even with sea water. These aquariums come in different sizes and shapes and are perfectly suitable for keeping all kinds of fishes.

*Plastic tanks* are just as durable as glass tanks. Plastic can be molded and fused without seams. If you want an aquarium without sharp edges and corners, choose a plastic tank. But the plastic should not be too thin; otherwise the water pressure will cause the walls to belly out, and the fish will appear distorted. If you want to photograph your fish, you should get a glass tank, because plastic walls always distort the image somewhat. Another drawback of plastic is that it scratches more easily than glass when improperly handled. You may ask why, given these disadvantages, anybody would buy a plastic tank. The answer is that a freestanding plastic tank with rounded edges and corners can look strikingly handsome. Molded *one-piece glass tanks* have gone out of style. One sees them occasionally used for breeding small fish species and as isolation tanks.

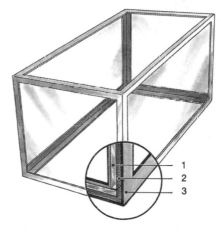

1 Glass wall,   2 Joint,   3 Aluminum frame

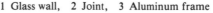

Frame tanks are available in many sizes and formats. The dealer will assist you in choosing.

# The Correct Aquarium

Since they have no seams they are easy to keep clean, but they hold only about 5 gallons (20 liters)* safely.

Internal stress factors in molded glass can cause larger tanks to crack or break. That is why all-glass tanks have to be protected from temperature changes. Also, the walls of these aquariums are not perfectly even and cause the fish to appear somewhat distorted.

Small all-glass tanks have been largely replaced by *tanks of transparent plastic* that are much lighter and less fragile than the earlier glass versions. (If the plastic should crack as a result of careless handling, it can be repaired with plastic glue.) The price of these plastic tanks is so low that any serious aquarist should have one as a quarantine or isolation tank (3 to 4 gallon [10–15 liter] capacity, equipped with heater and filter). It is best to buy this together with your main tank when you first start keeping fish.

One drawback of plastic tanks is that they are not scratch resistant. They should consequently be used only as a temporary substitute for the main tank, not as permanent display aquariums. On the other hand, these plastic tanks have an advantage of great practical value. They are narrower at the bottom than the top and can therefore be stacked for storage. Most devoted aquarists run out of space for their accessories and appre-

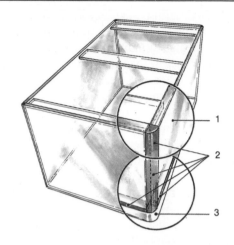

1 Glass wall,   2 Joints,   3 Styrofoam pad

Frameless all-glass tanks are adequate for all types of aquarium needs.

ciate that a stack of these small tanks takes up so little room.

**Advice for beginners:** Start out with a frameless glass tank.

## How to Restore Used Tanks

Beginners, especially children, are sometimes given an old aquarium by a friend or acquaintance. Often this will be an old-fashioned frame tank with glass panes cemented to the metal frame. The inside joints of these tanks should be sealed with silicone rubber. Use only silicone rubber with an acetic acid base for this purpose, and do not forget to seal the lower edge of the frame running along the top of the tank. Start by

---

* Comparable metric measurements are given in parentheses throughout the book.

removing all traces of grease from the glass with alcohol or an acetone solvent. Then squeeze the silicone rubber from the tube into the seams, smoothing it out with your finger if necessary. (Be sure you first coat your finger with dishwashing detergent so that the sealant will not stick to the finger.) A tank repaired in this way can still serve quite adequately for a number of years.

## Size and Format of the Tank

Most aquariums on the market are taller than they are wide. This is so, in part, because manufacturers take into account that the aquariums have to fit in with modern furniture. In addition, a narrow but tall tank offers a large viewing surface for a relatively low price.

But the greater the floor area of an aquarium, the healthier its inhabitants, both fish and plants. A large floor area offers you greater possibilities for arranging plants and otherwise decorating your aquarium, it allows bottom fish to stake out their territories, and lighting is more effective than in a tall and narrow aquarium.

Since distances appear shorter under water, any aquarium will appear narrower when it is filled with water, and the back of the tank will be clearly visible. Recently, some tank manufacturers have started producing tanks that are somewhat wider than they are tall, so that if you want an aquarium with a large floor area you no longer have to construct it yourself or have it custom-built.

The size of the tank is determined primarily by the size and number of the fish to be kept in it and their behavioral patterns. Do not start out with a tank that is too small, particularly if it is your first one. Novice aquarists like to buy fish, and a small tank is soon overpopulated. Also, a larger amount of water makes for a more stable biological environment that is more immune to the effects of mistakes in tank maintenance.

Important: The larger the aquarium, the safer the fish and the smaller the chance of unpleasant surprises for you. Before you buy equipment, give some thought to how many and what kind of fish you want to keep, and what size they grow to.

Large fish and/or fish with territorial behavior obviously need large aquariums, but small fish are not necessarily happy in a small tank. Many species of small fish live in schools of several thousands in their natural habitat, and they want company — preferably of their own kind — in the aquarium, too. A school should consist of at least seven to ten fish, and there should be adequate space for them to swim in. A school of fifty Neon Tetras moving gracefully through a well planted 3-foot (100-cm) tank is an unforgettable sight. The same fifty fish in a tank half that size are reminiscent of a crowd of shoppers in a bargain basement.

# The Correct Aquarium

Use the following rule of thumb to determine how much space aquarium occupants need: Estimate the length of the full-grown fish, and multiply each half inch (1 cm) by 1½ to 2 quarts (1½–2 liters). The result you get represents just the water and does not include the materials on the bottom of the tank or the plants, both of which also take up some space. But do not worry about the exact figure; in the course of time fish multiply, some die, and you buy new ones. The aquarium is, after all, a living world that is in constant flux.

One thing is obvious from our rule of thumb: Start out with as large an aquarium as you can afford.

Apart from the needs of the fish, you have to give some thought to the weight of the tank once it is filled with water.

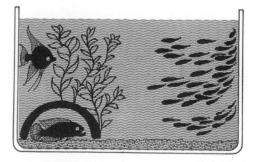

Remember when you buy your aquarium tank that the fish need sufficient space to thrive. Territorial fishes want caves or hiding places among plants; fishes living in schools should have an area of open water.

The weight of an aquarium is determined by its capacity, and the capacity is calculated by using the following formula:*

Capacity in gallons =
$$\frac{\text{Length} \times \text{width} \times \text{height (in inches)}}{231}$$

Since 1 gallon of water weighs about 9 pounds, an aquarium measuring 48 × 13 × 21 inches holds about 55 gallons and weighs about 500 pounds. Add to this about one quarter of the result for the weight of the bottom material and the decorations. In the above example, the filled and planted aquarium would weigh about 625 pounds. This does not include the weight of the stand or whatever piece of furniture the tank is to stand on. Some floors are not safe if they have to support 300 pounds (150 kg) per square yard (meter).

Important: If you are planning to get a large aquarium, you should consult an architect or builder to find out how much weight your floors can safely support. This is particularly important if you live in an upstairs apartment.

---

* A comparable formula using metric measurements would be:
Capacity in liters =
$$\frac{\text{length} \times \text{width} \times \text{height (in cm)}}{1000}$$
Since 1 liter of water weighs 1 kilogram, an aquarium measuring 100 × 40 × 50 cm holds 200 liters and weighs 200 kg. The filled aquarium would weigh about 250 kg.

# The Correct Aquarium

## The Cover

Most of the aquarium should be covered at the top with a piece of glass or plastic. This will keep the dust out and prevent the fish from jumping out. The cover should have one or more openings for heater or filter tubing and for feeding the fish. If you have a large aquarium, lifting the whole cover every time you need to clean it or want to feed the fish can be a nuisance. You may therefore want to have the cover cut into several panels that fit your tank exactly, and you can buy plastic runners for the panels. Then you can move the panels back and forth easily as needed. The cover panels should not make an air-tight barrier, but the cracks between them should never be so large that a fish could squeeze through.

## The Base

Before you set up your aquarium — preferably in a spot near one or more electrical outlets — you should make sure that the floor is perfectly level. If it is slanted, you have to even it out. The shelf, table top, or other piece of furniture on which the tank will stand, must also be stable enough not to bend under the weight of the full aquarium.

Some tanks can develop leaks, and you should therefore place a layer of felt or styrofoam under your aquarium.

Place the aquarium at a height that allows you to look at it comfortably from a sitting position.

# Water – The Natural Environment of Fish

Whether your fish and plants will thrive or not depends primarily on the composition of the water they live in. The quality of the water determines whether your fish will be healthy and prolific or whether they will be sickly and die.

Not all water is alike, and there is no such thing as chemically pure water in nature. Water contains gases, minerals, and organic matter from decaying leaves and wood and from plants and creatures living in the water.

## Gases Suspended in the Water

The presence of oxygen ($O_2$) and carbon dioxide ($CO_2$) is essential for all living things in the aquarium (see pages 37, 72). Fish and plants both absorb oxygen and give off carbon dioxide as they breathe. In addition, plants use sunlight energy to take carbon dioxide from their surroundings to make sugar, and they release oxygen in the process (see page 37). The number and kinds of fishes and plants in an aquarium determine whether a proper balance is naturally maintained or whether excess carbon dioxide has to be removed.

## Hardness of the Water

Water dissolves minerals from the earth it comes in contact with. Whether water is hard or soft depends on the amounts and types of minerals it contains. If it has a high mineral content, it is hard; if it is low in minerals, it is soft.

You can find out the mineral content of your tap water by asking your local water department, or you can measure it

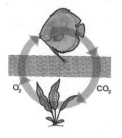

Oxygen and carbon dioxide exchange between fish and plants. During the day: The fish inhale oxygen and exhale carbon dioxide. In the photosynthetic process plants take up $CO_2$ and produce $O_2$.

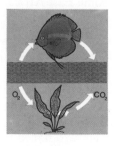

At night: In the dark plants cannot assimilate $CO_2$. Plants, as well as fish, inhale oxygen and release carbon dioxide.

# Water — The Natural Environment of Fish

yourself with indicator strips or with a test kit you can buy at the pet store. In heavily populated areas, water supply systems are often very complex, and the normal water source may occasionally be supplemented by water from a different area, water that is of different hardness and chemical composition. Your tap water may thus change suddenly, and you should check it periodically yourself.

In this book, the hardness of water is expressed by a "dH" scale beginning with 0. Each degree corresponds to 30 milligrams of calcium carbonate per 1 quart (1 liter) of water.

0–4 degrees dH = very soft
5–8 degrees dH = soft
9–12 degrees dH = medium hard
13 degrees dH and up = hard water

Since the soils of the areas tropical fish come from contain little or no calcium, these fish have adapted to very soft water. Only some East African Cichlids live in a natural environment of medium hard to hard water.

The water composition varies greatly in different parts of the country, and you should therefore either choose fish that are adapted to the kind of water you have or adjust the hardness of your water to the needs of the fish. You can buy distilled water and mix it with tap water to get the proper degree of hardness. This can be expensive in the long run. Rain water is often too polluted to be suitable for aquarium use. The only solution may be to buy an ion-exchanger, a device that removes minerals from the water and can produce soft, or even pure, water. What type of ion-exchanger you get depends on the quality of your tap water and the needs of your fish. Detailed information can be found in technical literature on aquariums and on the chemistry of water.

You may want to make soft water harder if your tap water is very soft and you want to keep live-bearing Toothed Carps or large Cichlids from Lakes Malawi and Tanganyika. To harden water, you use gypsum, but not the kind to patch walls with. Buy pure alabaster gypsum that is available at pet stores. Follow instructions on the product carefully, or consult books on water chemistry for aquariums.

## The Acidity of the Water

The acidity of the water is just as important as its mineral contents. Acidity is expressed in pH values. To explain the chemistry responsible for the acidity of water is beyond the scope of this little book. All natural water contains a certain amount of substances that react in either an alkaline or an acid fashion. Neutral water has a pH of 7. (Chemically pure water is also neutral, but it contains neither acid nor alkaline substances.) A pH below 7 means that the water is acid, above 7, that it is alkaline. Most tropical fish prefer a water pH of 5.8 to 7. Only the East African Cichlids need alkaline water (7.5 to 8.5 pH). If the water has a pH below 5.5 or above 9, the fish will show signs of ill health. The pH of your aquarium can be measured with test kits available at pet stores; indicator strips are not accurate enough for aquarium purposes.

## Humic Acid and Peat

The native waters where our aquarium fish come from are made acid by the presence of carbonic acid, dissolved carbon dioxide, and humic acid. Plants are able to absorb mineral nutrients and trace elements much better in combination with humic acid. Water in tropical areas often has considerably higher levels of humic acid than of carbonic acid. Humic acid maintains the acidity of the water better than carbonic acid because the latter fluctuates more with the metabolic action of water plants. The black-water rivers of the Amazon basin have high levels of humic acid, which accounts for the low pH of their water. In nature humic acid is produced by dead leaves, wood, and other plant matter in the water. We can introduce humic acid into the aquarium by circulating the water through peat filters or by adding liquid peat extract.

## Nitrogen Compounds

Fish excrete ammonia with their urine and feces. Decomposing animal proteins — fish food, dead snails, and dead fish — also produce ammonia. If you feed your fish by the spoonful, that is, if you overfeed them, you may be the main cause of excess ammonia, because the unused food will keep decomposing at the bottom of the tank. Ammonia is poisonous even at low concentrations. Fortunately, slightly acid water transforms ammonia into much less toxic ammonium. The following table gives the ammonia and ammonium concentrations of water at different pH levels.

| pH | % Ammonia | % Ammonium |
|----|-----------|------------|
| 6  | 0         | 100        |
| 7  | 1         | 99         |
| 8  | 4         | 96         |
| 9  | 25        | 75         |

Fish are therefore safe from ammonia poisoning as long as the pH stays around 5.8 to 7, even if some leftover food and other decaying matter is present. An aquarium that has not been cleaned for some time will have a fair amount of debris and old food in it, and the level of nitrogen compounds in the water will be high. If the water circulates through an acid-enhancing filter material such as peat, the ammonia will be converted into ammonium and the fish will be well. But

# Water – The Natural Environment of Fish

if the owner suddenly decides to attend to the long overdue chore of changing the water and replaces a third of it with tap water, he may find to his surprise that the fish are dying. Tap water is usually on the alkaline side and causes the pH in the aquarium to rise. This in turn causes ammonium to change to ammonia, and the fish die of ammonia poisoning.

Before these interconnections were properly understood, people thought (and some still think) that fish living in acid water could not tolerate a water change. All the old water was carefully saved. As long as there were just a few fish in the tank, they were not overfed, and there were plenty of plants, all would go well. It was in those days that devices were invented – still available today – for eliminating the cloudy debris without removing the water.

When we speak of "aged" water today, we mean water that has been in an aquarium with plants but no fish for several weeks and now provides a healthy environment for the fish. "Fresh" water means tap water that has sat for a while.

We know now that the East African Cichlids, used as they are to alkaline water, are in constant danger of ammonia poisoning if they are kept in dirty water. These fish are heavy feeders, and plants usually do not survive in their tanks. It is therefore important to equip their aquariums with especially powerful filters, and their water should be changed more frequently than that of other aquarium fishes.

The symptoms of ammonia poisoning resemble those of oxygen deficiency or excessively high levels of carbon dioxide. If the fish come to the surface and start gasping for air, you should therefore not automatically turn up the air pump but check the water first to see what is actually wrong.

A filter changes ammonia first into *nitrite* and then into *nitrate*. Nitrite is highly poisonous and must be transformed as quickly as possible. You should check the nitrite level every two weeks with a test kit, and if it is too high, you should clean the filter and change the water right away. An easy way to check is to smell the water. Nitrite makes it smell bad.

Nitrates are relatively harmless nitrogen salts, but they should not be allowed to accumulate. Our tap water usually contains more nitrates than tropical waters do, and too much nitrate harms the plants.

The transformation of ammonia into nitrite uses up a lot of oxygen. The less cloudy debris and old food there are in the tank, the less oxygen is used up and the more is available for the fish. All of the test kits mentioned in this section for checking water quality are available in pet stores.

**Advice for the beginner:** Check the water about every two weeks for pH, hardness, and nitrite level.

13

# *Water — The Natural Environment of Fish*

## From Tap Water to Aquarium Water

Our tap water is meant for human consumption. It is devoid of carbonic acid, i.e., carbon dioxide dissolved in water; and many important plant nutrients, such as phosphate, iron, and manganese have been removed from it. But due to pollution, our water does contain large amounts of nitrates, as well as traces of toxic substances and sometimes of heavy metals. In any case, we always have to feed aquarium plants, remove poisons from the water, and treat it before we place sensitive fish in it. Pet stores carry the appropriate devices and chemicals.

A new aquarium should be "dry run" for about two to three weeks, i.e., it should be set up, filled with water, planted, and the air pump, filter, etc. turned on, all without fish. This gives plants a chance to take root; filter bacteria can develop; and the water can turn into "good" aquarium water.

## The Native Waters of Our Aquarium Fishes

### South America

For the aquarist, the Amazon region is the most fascinating area of South America. This is the home of our most beautiful aquarium fishes, such as Neon Tetras, Discus Fish, Angelfish (Scalares), Armored Corydoras, and Dwarf Cichlids.

Three types of water have evolved in the rivers of this region:

*White water,* which is found in the main branch of the Amazon River, for instance, is cloudy, yellow, and clayey. It is soft (0.6 to 1.2 dH), slightly acid (pH 6.5 to 6.9), and contains minute amounts of ammonium and nitrate.

*Clear water* is transparent and yellow to dark olive green in color. It is extremely soft (0.3 to 0.8 dH), somewhat more acid than "white water" (pH 4.6 to 6.6), and contains hardly any ammonium or nitrate.

*Black water,* which is transparent and dark brown, is found in the Rio Negro. It is even softer (0 to 0.1 dH) and more acid (3.8 to 5.3 pH) than "clear water," and it also contains practically no ammonium or nitrate.

There is, of course, no clear line separating these three types of water, and most of our decorative fishes come from areas where black water mixes with white or clear water. Pure black water is not a viable environment, and it is unlikely that any fish species have adapted to it.

The rest of South America does not have such distinct types of water. South American water is generally soft to medium hard and slightly acid.

### Central America

The Cyprinodonts or live-bearing Toothed Carps come from this area. They live in medium hard to hard water

# *Water — The Natural Environment of Fish*

that is neutral or slightly alkaloid. Some are also found in brackish water.

### Africa

Many egg-laying Cyprinodonts, as well as Characins and Cichlids, are found in West Africa, where they live in waters that are fairly rich in minerals. The rivers of Central and West Africa generally have slightly acid water with low mineral content. The Stanley Pool in the Congo River, for instance, has a hardness of 2 dH, a pH of 6.5, and practically no ammonium or nitrate. The East African lakes Tanganyika and Malawi are the home of mouthbreeding Cichlids. These fish have recently become very popular. They live in harder, alkaline waters. Lake Tanganyika has water of 10 dH and a pH of 7.5 to 9.2. In aquariums they have been bred for years in water of 17 dH and a pH of 8.2. They can even tolerate water as hard as 25 dH.

### Southeast Asia

The Danios come from southern India and Ceylon. The water in these areas is very soft (0.2 to 0.7 dH) and practically neutral. The Malayan Archipelago is the home of more aquarium fishes than any other part of the world except South America. The water here is almost free of minerals and very clean; it has a dH of 0.6 and a pH of 6.0.

All these figures are only averages based on samples taken from various rivers at different times, and they do not reflect seasonal changes. In the flood plains of the Rio Negro, for example, the water level rises as much as thirty feet above normal during the rainy season — and that over an area of thousands of square miles.

But a survey of tropical waters can give us a few useful pointers for keeping fish. If you want to keep fish without breeding them, they will tolerate harder and more alkaline water than they are used to. If they are to breed successfully, however, they need water like that of their native habitat to which they have adapted over millions of years.

# *Aquarium Equipment and Accessories*

## Heater and Thermostat

In order to keep tropical fish and plants at temperatures they are used to, you have to heat the water to about 73° to 79°F (23°–26°C), sometimes higher. This is done by means of an aquarium heater, which consist of a heating coil inside a glass tube filled with sand. The heat can be regulated with a thermostat.

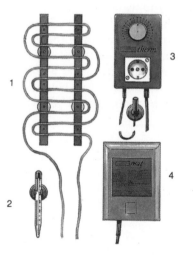

Bottom heater with accessories:
1 Heating cable mounted on plastic runners,
2 Thermometer, 3 Thermostat with heat sensor,
4 Transformer.

There are *electric rod-type heaters* without thermostats, and *automatic heaters* with built-in thermostats. If you buy a thermostat separately, you will find some that are designed for placing inside the aquarium and others that are to be mounted on the outside of the tank. Purists who do not like the looks of technical apparatus inside the tank can build a heater into the outside filtering equipment. It is up to you to choose the heater that best suits your aquarium and your pocketbook.

We strongly recommend automatic temperature control, whether in the form of an automatic heater or a thermostat separate from the heating unit. Tropical fish do not tolerate changes in water temperature well, and the water should stay within 2°F (1°C) of the temperature set on the thermostat. The heating unit itself should not be too powerful. The normally recommended capacity of one watt per liter is too high for the usual temperatures in our living rooms. It would be needed only if the aquarium were in an unheated room. In a room with temperatures of 68° to 73°F (20°–23°C), a heating capacity of 0.3 to 0.5 watt per quart (liter) is sufficient because the tank has to be heated only a

Characins
Upper left: Flame Tetra *(Hyphessobrycon flammeus)*; Upper right: Bleeding Heart Tetra ▷
*(Hyphessobrycon erythrostigma)*. Middle left: False Rummy-Nose *(Petitella georgiae)* at top and Rummy-Nose *(Hemigrammus rodostomus)* at bottom; Middle right: Callistus Tetra *(Hyphessobrycon callistus)*. Lower left: Brown-Tailed Pencilfish *(Nannostomus eques)*; Lower right: Striped Headstander *(Anostomus anostomus)*.

few degrees above the temperature of the room. At the wattage we recommend, the fish are not going to be too cold, especially since the lighting usually helps heat the aquarium, too. Of course, you also check the temperature with a thermometer (see page 28), and on hot days you may want to shut off the light if the water is getting too warm.

A less powerful heater is not only cheaper to buy and to run, it also has another advantage. Most thermostats are equipped with a heat sensor with a bimetal contact. A powerful heater turns on and off constantly, and the contact soon gets worn. It starts to stick, and before you know it, it will refuse to open at all, perhaps causing the whole aquarium to turn into bouillabaisse overnight. A small heater is easier on the thermostat and heats the aquarium more slowly. Even if the thermostat should go on the blink, you have time to intervene before the water gets too hot.

The heaters described so far heat only the tank. But all aquarium plants like to have "warm feet," and nurseries specializing in water plants therefore recommend keeping the bottom temperature about one degree centigrade above the water temperature. To *heat the bottom,* you place a waterproof heating cable (approved for such use) on the bottom of the tank in S-curves (see drawing on page 16). It should be mounted on plastic tracks or feet so that it does not touch the glass, or it can be incorporated into the bottom gravel. The same result can be achieved with a heating pad that is placed directly underneath the aquarium and separated from the supporting surface by adequate insulation materials. If the heating pad is too strong or improperly installed, it can cause glass damage.

Since warm water rises to the top, fresh water will constantly flow through the bottom material if a bottom heater is used. This prevents organic matter from rotting on the bottom, brings nutrients to plant roots, and causes the bottom gravel to act as an additional filter. Water quality is significantly improved, and the entire aquarium climate becomes more stable.

A heating pad or heating cables may be able to heat the aquarium without the aid of another heater inside the tank. But the bottom heating unit should not be too strong. One watt for about 10 quarts (10 liters) is sufficient to circulate the entire water mass through the bottom gravel once or twice a day. We therefore favor the use of a dual-circuit thermostat that constantly regulates the bottom heat and can also control an aquarium heater that is turned on during cold days.

We mentioned above that the bottom gravel can act as an additional filter if the water circulates through it constantly. But any filter gets dirty and clogged after a while, and if you use bottom heat, you should clean the gravel every year or two.

# *Aquarium Equipment and Accessories*

Heaters and thermostats are electrical appliances that function underwater. This can create some problems. They must be UL-approved for safety, but it is still possible to get an electric shock if, for example, a heater in the tank is damaged and you happen to reach into the aquarium to clip a plant or clean the

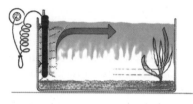

Aquarium with poor water circulation: Warm water moves up only while the heater is on. There is always a layer of cold water just above the floor. Circulation is so slow that hot and cold water do not mix.

Aquarium with good water circulation: Bottom heating causes freshly warmed water to rise constantly, and cold and warm water mix quickly.

glass. You usually cannot tell when a fish gets a shock. Electrical mishaps occur only rarely, but they are unpleasant and you do well to try and prevent them. Check for commercially available electronic safety devices that eliminate all risks. They are installed between the outlet and the unit and shut off the current if there is any malfunction.

**Advice to the beginner:** A heating rod together with a thermostat are adequate for a start.

## Optimal Lighting

Some aquarium plants and fishes like bright sunlight, while others prefer shade, but all need light and the cycle of day and night to thrive. The aquarium therefore needs lighting.

Some older books, and even some recent ones, recommend placing the aquarium next to a window so that it will receive as much daylight as possible. But natural light cannot be controlled. Even if the aquarium is next to a north window, green algae may form during the summer and turn the water opaque, and in the winter the plants will wither because it is too dark for them and because our rhythm of day and night is not the same as in the tropics.

We know that animals as well as plants are equipped with internal clocks that determine their normal daily and seasonal behavior. Light is an important

# Aquarium Equipment and Accessories

biological time-keeper for all of them. Some species of fish, for example, spawn immediately after sunrise, and some only hunt at dusk. The growth spurts of many plants and the spawning periods of most fish are regulated by the length of day, which in our latitudes changes in the course of the year. Near the equator a day is always twelve hours long. A tropical aquarium should therefore be lighted about twelve to thirteen hours to approximate a tropical day. To avoid fluctuations you may want to purchase a timer that turns the light on and off automatically.

Besides the duration of daylight, light intensity is important for all organisms. An aquarium needs lighting that supplies sufficient light for tropical plants and that creates light of a color that resembles daylight. Fish generally need less light than plants.

Even today many aquarists do not have adequate lighting. Water acts as a light filter; and brown, peat-filtered water absorbs even more light than regular water. Large, rapidly growing aquarium plants are least affected. Their leaves are close enough to the water's surface that they are able to assimilate sufficient light. Smaller plants, such as *Echinodorus tenellus,* which grows to no more than four inches (10 cm) and is usually planted in the lowest areas of the tank to form a kind of meadow, have the whole length of the water column above them and therefore receive too little light.

The ideal amount of light for aquarium plants is 0.4 to 0.7 watts per quart (liter) of water. An aquarium measuring 48 × 12 × 21 inches (100 × 50 × 40 cm), holding 55 gallons (200 liters) of water, should have a lamp of about 80 to 140 watts.

Correct aquarium lighting: The fish, orienting itself by gravity and by the light entering from above, is properly positioned on a vertical axis.

Incorrect aquarium lighting: If the light enters from the side, the fish gets two different signals for "up." The fish is positioned on a slanted axis.

# Aquarium Equipment and Accessories

But in such tropical conditions, algae grow so rapidly that you should include some algae-eating fish in your aquarium right away, such as the Siamese Flying Fox *(Epalzeorhynchus siamensis),* the Sphenops Molly *(Poecilia sphenops),* some kind of Bristle-Nose *(Ancistrus),* or the Chinese Algae-Eater *(Gyrinocheilus aymonieri).*

It is impossible to give an exact light intensity for fish, but in a well-planted aquarium they have the opportunity to find shady places if the light is too bright for them. The closer the color of the lighting is to that of sunlight, the more "natural" fish and plants will appear. But in nature, too, the color of light varies. In the morning and evening, sunlight contains a lot of red and appears "warm." At midday, it contains a lot of blue and appears "cold." Red light encourages vertical growth in plants; blue light furthers sturdiness. Red and blue have to be supplied in the correct proportions by the aquarium lighting.

## Which Lights Are Best?

Light bulbs are hardly used anymore for lighting tanks. While their light spectrum feels comfortable to the human eye, their light emission is small, they are too expensive to use, and they give off too much heat. Most aquariums are now lighted with *fluorescent tubes.* These are more efficient than light bulbs, and you can combine several types of tubes with variously colored light to achieve a pleasant light mixture that suits the needs of plants. There are "warm-tone" fluorescent lights using the higher, red end of the spectrum and "cold-tone" lights with a lot of blue. Then there are "white" fluorescent lights, containing all the colors of the spectrum like daylight, and violet "grow lights" that stimulate plant growth. An aquarium should have a combination of one warm-tone and one cold-tone fluorescent tube or one warm-tone and one daylight fluorescent tube. You can add grow lights if you want luxuriant plants, but they tend to change the color of the fish; red fish particularly do not look quite natural. These grow lights should not be installed until three to six months after the aquarium has been set up because otherwise they may cause blue-green algae to form.

Fluorescent lights lose half of their power within six months. Aquarists who care about healthy plant growth should replace them every six months. Be particularly meticulous about this if you use grow lights.

The sizes and intensities of fluorescent tubes are standardized. Check with your local retailer for availability and selection.

Beginners can easily start with smaller fluorescent tubes and grow undemanding plants such as *Sagattaria* or *Elodea.*

# Aquarium Equipment and Accessories

These plants are so hardy that they do well even with little light and will withstand the mistakes a beginner is likely to make. Several hardy species of *Cryptocoryne* also tolerate shade (see page 38). Ask for advice at your pet store if you are in doubt about what to get.

If after some experimenting you would like to keep more demanding plants that require more light, you can acquire stronger lights then. If, on the other hand, you take a fancy to large Cichlids, herbivorous Characins, or fish living in brackish water, your plants will soon disappear, and normal lighting will be quite sufficient. There will be enough light for your fish in any case. Most lights are equipped with reflectors which increase the light intensity. If this is not the case, you should line the cover with foil to achieve the same effect. You may also find fluorescent tubes with a reflector coating. Ask your retailer.

Light will be used more efficiently if you clean the cover of the tank every week. Water splashing up causes mineral deposits, and in time green algae will begin to form. A dozen fluorescent tubes will be ineffective if they are expected to provide light through a dirty cover.

Fluorescent tubes may be placed on or hung above the aquarium. If it is feasible to hang the lights from the ceiling, that is best. Hanging lamps do not heat the water in the tank. They are also out of the way of splashing, and there is less chance of malfunctioning. Access to the tank is facilitated if there are no lights resting on the cover, and some jobs like catching fish or emptying the tank are much easier. If you first have to move the lights aside, you cannot see well what you are doing. The distance between the lights and the tank cover should be about 4 inches (10 cm). When you need to do work in the tank, you can raise them by shortening the cords or chains from which they hang.

*Mercury vapor lights,* which are suspended over the aquarium from the ceiling, are a recent innovation that seems to be overwhelmingly successful. They should, however, only be used with tanks that are 20 inches (50 cm) or higher. Their yield is much higher than that of other types of lighting, and they are therefore economical to use. The bulbs last much longer than fluorescent tubes. After two years of use, they still have 80% of their original capacity. This more than makes up for the higher initial investment. These lights reach their full intensity only about five minutes after being turned on. This gradual lighting up, which is more like a real sunrise, is easier on the occupants of the aquarium who are often startled by the sudden change from dark to light. The light of these lamps is so intense that plants will grow out of the tank unless they are cut back.

Nurseries specializing in water plants

recommend that the backs and sides of very large aquariums be planted very densely and the tank be left open at the top. Then, when the water level is lowered about an inch (a few centimeters) below normal, a cover will probably be needed only on the forward half. (Fish hardly ever jump in areas with dense plant growth.) In such an aquarium the leaves of marsh plants, such as *Cryptocoryne, Aponogeton, Echinodorus,* and *Limnophila* grow out of the water, and some plants may even flower. An open aquarium like this can improve the environment we live in, since central heating dries out the air in our rooms.

## Filters and Their Care

Every aquarium should have an efficient filter that is in constant use. A filter removes leftover food, fish excreta, and decaying plant material from the water and thus improves its quality. It also makes the water look clean, but that is relatively unimportant. Water with some debris suspended in it is far less harmful than crystal-clear water that is overloaded with waste products.

### Types of Filters

Most filters designed to be placed inside the tank are adequate for small aquariums. They are also used in breeding and quarantine tanks. There are also

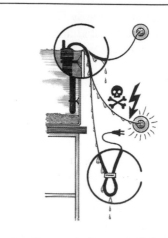

*Correct and incorrect placement of electric cord: Water can spill from a full tank and run down along the cord into the electrical outlet, causing a short. If you do not have an outlet above the water level, make a loop in the cord so that the water can drip off.*

larger filters of this type that can be used if outside filters are undesirable. Inside filters can be hidden behind plants and decorative objects without adverse effect on their functioning. Cleaning inside filters is always upsetting for the fish, but there are now some new types available with cassettes of filter material that can be exchanged without taking the entire filter unit out of the water. Inside filters are usually operated with an air pump.

*Outside filters* are used if you do not want to have a clutter of gadgets inside the aquarium. They can be out of sight if they are mounted behind the tank or placed in an enclosed cabinet below it. Outside filters do not take up space in

24

# Aquarium Equipment and Accessories

the aquarium and can therefore be larger than inside filters, which means that they filter more efficiently. Small outside filters are run by air pumps, larger ones with water pumps. The latter suck the water of the aquarium through a filter container with various filter materials. These filters not only clean the water but also create a strong current. They are ideal for tanks more than 30 inches (80 cm) long that are designed more with the needs of fish in mind than those of plants. These siphoning filters are essential for heavily populated aquariums.

Filters are divided according to their method of functioning into biological slow filters and mechanical fast filters.

In a *biological slow filter* bacteria and algae form on the filtering material one to two weeks after placement in the tank. These organisms break down the waste products of fish into relatively non-toxic nitrates which are then removed as the water is exchanged. The greater the surface area on which bacteria can form, the more efficient the filter. Bacteria need oxygen to survive, and consequently as much as possible of the filter material should be in contact with water high in oxygen.

Because the breakdown of nitrogen compounds into nitrate uses up oxygen, water will become more and more deficient the deeper it penetrates into the filter. In many filters where the water is filtered from top to bottom (or vice

versa) through layers of filter materials, only the first 2 to 4 inches (5–10 cm) have enough bacteria to activate breakdown. It is best to use filters where the water passes through a filtering mass about 2 inches (5 cm) thick and with a large surface area. *Under-gravel filtration* also yields good results. Here water is pumped underneath a grate placed on the bottom of the aquarium. Bottom heating causes the water to flow up through the gravel from below. Aquarium filters should be large enough that the entire water mass passes through the filter every hour. Pump efficiency can drop up to fifty percent depending on the filter medium used and the amount of dirt in the filter. Take this reduction of power into account when you calculate the pumping capacity you need. Again, let the expert at the pet store advise you.

*Mechanical fast filters* are water pumps with small filter inserts designed for removing larger particles or debris floating in the water. They are used for short periods to clear the water after major maintenance chores. They are also useful as supplementary filters for heavily populated tanks or for aquariums with Cichlids or other strong feeders and burrowers. But they are no substitute for biological slow filters or the regular changing of water.

Because a clogged filter is no longer effective and only overloads the pump, the filter material needs to be washed or

# Aquarium Equipment and Accessories

replaced frequently. If the filter insert has not been cleaned for some time, bacteria form on it, and it turns into a biological slow filter. But since the surface area is small and the material full of dirt, the harm due to decaying particles far outweighs the benefits of slow filtering.

**Filter Materials**

All commonly used materials filter large dirt particles from the water mechanically, and they can also provide a surface for bacteria to grow on. Some filter media alter the water chemically, and others remove harmful substances from the water. Coarse gravel and fine clay tubes function primarily as mechanical filters but also encourage the growth of bacteria. Polyester fiber and foam filter out small particles suspended in the water. They are easy to clean and are frequently used in mechanical fast filters. Activated charcoal draws toxic substances from the aquarium water. A charcoal filter must be used when medication is to be removed from the water, when water becomes cloudy as a result of excess feeding, and after a large fish or a number of snails have died. But since these substances soon break down further in a charcoal filter, it should be removed after three or four days. You should always have some spare charcoal on hand for emergencies. When a tank is newly set up, fresh tap water can first be filtered through charcoal to remove harmful chemical substances. Peat acidifies the water and gives off humic acid.

**Care of a Filter**

How long a filter is used and how often it should be cleaned depends on the product, the quality of the water, the size and number of fish, and the type of food they receive. New biological filters take two to three months before they become fully effective and should be left in the aquarium as long as possible. If, however, the tank is overcrowded and the fish overfed, a biological filter may need to be cleaned frequently, but then it will be nothing more than a mechanical filter. Mechanical filters must be changed or cleaned as soon as the filter unit becomes slimy and the flow through it is reduced. Charcoal should be replaced every three or four days. Because hot water kills bacteria, the filters must be washed in cold or lukewarm water (about 86°F [30°C]).

Important: If the pump stops, causing the water flow through the filter to be interrupted or the water to flow out of the filter, the filter must be cleaned thoroughly. The bacteria die in the absence of oxygen and poison the water. All the fish in the aquarium may die within a short period of time if the contents of the filter are washed into the tank.

Even the best of filters cannot keep the

water clean and liveable forever. It may convert ammonia into nitrites and then into nitrates, but in high concentrations nitrates, too, are harmful (see page 43). Filters cannot substitute for changing the water (see page 67).

Healthy aquarium plants are as effective in keeping the water clean as filters. Algae and bacteria settle on their leaves, and plants feed on ammonium, nitrite, and nitrate; give off oxygen; and help remove carbon dioxide. Do not underestimate the contribution of plants to the general health of an aquarium.

**Advice to the beginner:** Buy the aquarium and the filter at the same time. The salesperson will be able to tell you how to take care of the filter.

## Aeration

Filters not only clean the water; they also keep it moving. This is important because all our aquarium fish originally lived in water that moves. Even stagnant water is acted on by wind so that it is never as still as the water in an aquarium. In a tank without filter and aeration, a layer of bacteria forms at the water's surface, a kind of skin that impedes the essential exchanges between air and water. Because the breakdown of nitrogen requires a lot of oxygen, the water that comes out of the filter is oxygen-depleted and saturated with carbon diox-

ide, and when water is overloaded with carbon dioxide, the fish suffocate. That is why it is essential to get rid of the carbon dioxide. This is done by installing the filter in such a way that the outlets are exactly at the water surface. Then the filtered water is in direct contact with the air, gives off carbon dioxide, and

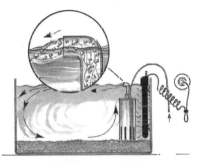

Biological inside filter. The smaller the air bubbles emerging from the filter outlet, the greater the mass of water moved and the more thorough the circulation in the tank.

carries oxygen into the aquarium. Water pump filters also have jets that dissipate the stream of water and thus promote the exchange of gases. If your filter is run by an air pump, you can also aerate the water with an airstone (see drawing on page 29). The air is driven through the stone by the air pump. The many small air bubbles that come out of the airstone have a much large surface area than a few large bubbles. The exchange of gases between water and air is increased because water can absorb oxygen only

# Aquarium Equipment and Accessories

where it is in direct contact with the air. The smaller the bubbles from the airstone, the more oxygen is released into the water. Airstones should be replaced periodically since after some time of use they get clogged and start to discharge larger air bubbles, as well as causing the pump to work harder.

Arrange the airstone and filter outlets in such a way that all of the water is mixed evenly and there are no warm and cool spots. By sprinkling a little debris or wet peat on the water you will be able to tell how the water moves in your tank and how to make improvements if necessary.

If your aquarium contains few fish and a lot of plants, you can dispense with aeration and the dispersion of the filter effluvium because the plants will take up all the carbon dioxide. An ideal relationship like this between fish and plants is most likely to exist in a so-called Dutch aquarium, which is essentially a botanical underwater garden where fish are present primarily to animate the underwater landscape.

A regular community aquarium is usually just the opposite. Fish outnumber the plants, and the plants, often covered with algae, barely survive. Such a tank has to be well aerated. (It would be better, of course, to divide the fish into three separate tanks.) Tanks with plant-eating fish have to have strong aeration.

An aquarium that contains a lot of fish and few or no plants needs strong aeration. It should not be covered tightly because carbon dioxide has to be able to escape. A Dutch aquarium, on the other hand, needs a tight cover to keep the carbon dioxide in the tank for the plants.

Aquariums with fish from fast-moving water must always be equipped with a water pump, and sometimes an airstone is needed as well.

## Useful Accessories

You can buy all sorts of other accessories and decorative items for your aquarium. Many of them are quite unnecessary, but some of them you do need.

In order to regulate the temperature in an aquarium with tropical fish, you need a *thermometer.* Some have suction cups so that they can be attached to the wall, and others are meant to be stuck in the bottom gravel.

You also need attachments for your filter and aeration systems. Air pumps move the air through plastic tubes to the filters and airstones, and clamps and valves are needed to regulate the flow of air. These items should be made of plastic, not metal. Never use brass clamps. Brass forms verdigris, which will at some point get into the aquarium and is extremely poisonous to fish.

Manufacturers of large filters and water pumps also market accessories,

# Aquarium Equipment and Accessories

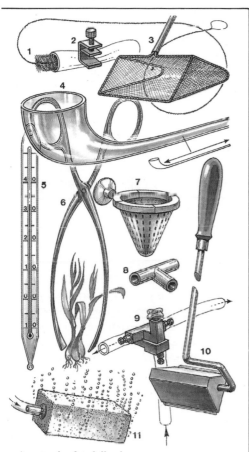

Accessories for daily chores:
1 Bottle brush for tubes and hoses
2 Hose clamp
3 Fish net
4 Glass trap
5 Thermometer
6 Plant tongs
7 Food strainer
8 T-hose
9 T-hose with valve regulating air flow
10 Window washer
11 Airstone

such as special pipe and hose brushes, for their products. Ask your pet store dealer for information.

You can buy *tubifex strainers* and *feeding rings*. They are installed in a corner of the aquarium to prevent dry food from spreading all over the aquarium. The tubifex strainers keep tubifex (sludge worms) and red mosquito larvae from drifting to the bottom and digging into the gravel. These devices have not proved too successful in practice.

The simplest way to catch fish is to use a *fish net*. Get as large a one as you can manipulate in your tank. With a small net you have to chase after the fish more actively, thus upsetting all the fish, as well as injuring the plants. Catching fish with a *glass trap* creates less of a disturbance in the tank. With their lateral-line sense organs the fish feel something approaching, but they cannot tell what it is. You can also use a net to drive the fish into the glass trap.

*Plant tongs* are used to plant and thin plants, as well as to remove rocks, snails, and dead fish.

Finally, there are gadgets that facilitate cleaning the tank. To syphon off old food and to change the water, you need a *hose* about 5 feet (1.5 m) long and ½ to ¾ inch (1–2 cm) in diameter. If your tap water is suitable for aquarium use (see page 10), you can buy a piece of hose long enough to reach from sink to aquarium, with an attachment at one end to clamp on the faucet. Large aquariums are easier to fill with a hose; this saves you carrying heavy buckets. You also need at least two *buckets* that cannot be used for household cleaning. Even small traces of soap and detergents are highly poisonous for fish. With waterproof magic markers write on the buckets "Aquarium" in large letters, and tell your family how important it is not to use the buckets for any other purpose. Watering cans or buckets with spouts are better than plain ones because they are easier to pour from.

To clean the front panel of the tank you can use a *window wiper* with a felt or razor edge but without brass parts. If you handle a razor carelessly, you may

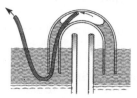

What to do when an air bubble blocks the water flow in a U-shaped hose: Insert a smaller hose and suck out the air . . .

. . . or add a T-nose at the highest point of the U to allow the air to escape. Clamp off the tube while the apparatus is running.

scratch the glass, which is particularly undesirable if you want to take photos of your fish. Wipers with a sponge on one side and some scratchy material on the other are safer. Most algae can be wiped off with the foam rubber side; and the tougher algae, as well as the calcium deposits, will give way to scrubbing with the rough side of the wiper. There are also window wipers with magnets. One magnet is placed against the glass on the inside of the tank; the other is moved over the glass on the outside, pulling along the inside magnet, which cleans as it moves.

Important: Many *plastics* making up household utensils as well as decorative objects release phenol or other substances that are toxic for fish. Polypropylenes and synthetic materials containing so-called softeners are particularly dangerous. The softeners are gradually washed out by water; the synthetic material first feels a little sticky and eventually becomes hard and brittle. Any object that still smells of plastic after having been placed in hot water for several hours is out of the question for aquarium use. Hard PVC (polyvinyl chloride) may be used in an aquarium after it has been washed in a 15% to 20% acetic acid solution to remove the toxic top layer. Do not forget to neutralize or at least dilute the acid with soda before you pour it out; otherwise it may corrode the plumbing.

# Setting Up and Decorating the Aquarium

Once you have placed the tank on a level surface and installed the necessary equipment, you can begin to decorate your aquarium.

## The Back Wall

You do not have to decorate the back wall, but fish seem to feel safer when one wall is protected. Also, the aquarium appears deeper and more peaceful if no light enters from the back. The simplest solution is to paint the back wall black or gray on the outside. You can also compose a backdrop by gluing bark, wood, glass, etc. on cardboard, which you then mount behind the aquarium. But as the back wall gets covered by algae, decorations gradually vanish from sight unless you clean the glass frequently, and that is not desirable because it disturbs the fish too much.

By decorating the back wall with varied materials you not only introduce additional surfaces where algae — which fish consider a delicacy and feed on — can establish themselves, but you also supply hiding places for less aggressive and newly hatched fish.

If you want to, you can remove the back wall altogether and build a natural-looking backdrop out of rocks and sand. Do not use cement because it is poisonous for freshwater fish. Instead, pour freshly mixed epoxy between and all over the rocks to make everything stick together well. It should have a natural look when assembled. Then you can pour sand over it all to give the surface an even color and coat everything with one more layer of epoxy, which will harden within about an hour. This kind of back wall is quite heavy.

You can also buy back walls made of polyurethane which are quite light. These must be glued or taped to the tank until they have soaked up sufficient water. These back walls are sold in thick sheets that the aquarist can then shape to his liking by digging out caves and hollows and building up protrusions. These polyurethane walls can be glued to the glass in the back, or they can be mounted in such a way that they can be taken out. Be sure there is no space between backdrop and glass where fish could get caught.

## Floor Covering and Rocks

The bottom material and rocks should contain no calcium. Most fishes want soft water, and calcium makes water hard. You can buy gravel and sand of different coarseness. Plants like sand of 1 to 2 millimeters diameter. Finer sand prevents good water circulation. Coarser gravel allows debris to sift through to the bottom where it cannot be siphoned off. The bottom material should be at least 2 to 3 inches (5–8 cm) thick and as much

# Setting Up and Decorating the Aquarium

thicker as you like in larger aquariums.

If you have a small tank, you can buy the gravel at the pet store. If you need one hundred pounds or more, it will be cheaper to buy at a builder's supply store. Be sure to ask for quartz gravel. Pre-washed sand or gravel will save you a lot of time and effort. All gravel has to be washed before it can be used in the tank. Fill a bucket up to about one quarter with gravel, add water, stir vigorously, and pour out the water. Repeat the process until the water is almost clear. Washed gravel has to be rinsed three to five times, unwashed gravel at least twice as many times.

Quartz gravel has the disadvantage of being light in color and reflecting the light that enters the tank from the top. But many fishes, especially those from the black-water regions, like dim light.

There are also various darker, calcium-free gravels available at pet stores. Some are made up of reddish to dark brown lava, but this kind of gravel is quite abrasive and therefore not suited for bottom dwellers.

Decorative rocks for fresh-water tanks should always consist of calcium-free, igneous rock, such as granite, gabbro, or basalt, that was formed from the magma in the earth's interior. Most slate is also safe. Sediment rock may or may not be calcium-free and should be checked out before it is introduced into a fresh-water aquarium. Limestone, such as marble, is never to be used in an aquarium. Pieces of reddish brown lava are the best kind of decorative stone. This type of lava is porous and therefore relatively light, and it is available in all kinds of sizes and shapes. Even someone who is quite indifferent to fish will exclaim with delight when shown an aquarium in which a dark polyurethane backdrop, reddish sand, and lava rocks set off green plants and colorful fish to their best advantage.

Of course, the rocks must be thoroughly scrubbed before they are put in the tank.

If you collect your own rocks and gravel, be sure to test whether they contain calcium. You do this by placing a drop of hydrochloric acid on a sample. If there is any calcium, bubbles will form.

You can arrange gravel and rocks to achieve nice visual effects. The bottom material should be shallowest at the front and rise up toward the back. A terraced floor looks more interesting than a flat bottom. Terraces made up of rows of stones do not stay in place for long. The motion of the water and of the fish causes the gravel between the stones to slide out and the whole floor to flatten. Flagstones stood on end work better. PVC strips that can be glued to the bottom of the tank and then covered with stones and gravel or terraces molded out of polyurethane last longest.

If you want strong and healthy plants, this is the time to add fertilizer to the bottom gravel, but you can do this only if you do not plan to get burrowing fishes.

## Wood and Other Decorative Materials

At the pet store you can buy tree roots and driftwood that have been immersed in water or lain in a bog so long that there is nothing left that could rot. This wood must first be boiled in water until it becomes saturated and will no longer float to the surface. Tree roots are the favorite haunts of catfish and other fish that like to hide. Fishes with suction mouths often hang on to driftwood pieces even when you lift them out of the water. Cave-dwelling fishes also like coconut shells, but these, too, must be boiled before use. If you want to use flower pots for bottom-dwelling fishes, you must soak the new pots at least one day in 2 gallons (10 liters) of water and 2 handfuls of peat. The humic acid from the peat binds the aluminum that may have been added in the manufacturing process. Old clay pots need not be soaked.

If you fit the decorations to the needs of the fish, the well-being of the tank's occupants will be enhanced. If you plan to have fishes with territorial behavior patterns, it makes sense to build some partitions out of stones to mark ter-

ritorial borders. Behind these walls weaker fish can get out of sight of the more aggressive ones. In an all-open aquarium the biggest fish would soon terrorize all the others. If, on the other hand, you keep fish that travel in schools, they need a large swimming area, and most of the decorations should be at the back of the tank.

Scalares need large driftwood roots and tall plants to hide in, whereas bottom fish like to dwell among rocks. If you have burrowing fishes, the lowest rock of a stone structure should rest directly on the floor of the tank so that the fish cannot burrow underneath and topple the whole thing. Labyrinth fishes need floating plants to build their nests in.

An aquarium looks most attractive when the decorations provide some variety. A lot of little stones set off a large rock to advantage, and a single large plant growing among small ones stands out in dramatic contrast. A decorative rock and a piece of driftwood make a lovely centerpiece in a meadow of water grasses.

## Filling the Tank with Water

When you have finished decorating, you can start filling the tank with water. If you want to have plants, fill the tank about one third full before you plant them. This prevents leaves and stems from drying out. When you pour in the water, make sure not to stir up the gravel, especially if you added fertilizer. A good way to do this is to place a large plate in the tank and slowly pour the water on it with a watering can, hose, or jug. If you fill the tank directly from the faucet, you have to watch out that the hose does not slip out of the tank. Squeeze it between the tank and the cover. And do not try to do anything else while the tank is filling. Do not start reading a detective story or put the children to bed while the water is running. Tanks have a way of spilling over the instant you forget about them. Do not even answer the phone!

# *Aquarium Plants*

## Short Introduction to Plants

With the exception of ferns and moss, aquarium plants are flowering plants with roots, stems, leaves, and blossoms. Plants that grow natively in still waters tend to be delicate; those growing in fast-moving water are more robust. Remember when you take your plants home that water plants do not have a protective coating on their leaves that keeps them from drying out. Even the slightest dehydration will inevitably make them wither.

In order to live, plants must be able to breathe continuously. In this process, they use up oxygen and produce carbon dioxide. They are also characterized by the photosynthetic mode of nutrition; i.e., with the aid of energy from sunlight and of chlorophyll, they absorb water, minerals, and carbon dioxide and turn them into sugar, which is then converted into starches and cellulose. In this process, oxygen is set free. Plants produce more oxygen than they need themselves only if they have enough light and carbon dioxide. In the dark or with insufficient lighting, plants use up oxygen without producing it and therefore compete with the fish for oxygen.

## Water Plants

Water plants like *Egeria densa* have totally adapted to life in water and can no longer live on land. Their roots serve less for absorbing nutrients than for holding on to the ground. Sometimes the plants dispense with roots altogether and just float in the water. The leaves are extremely thin and feathered to increase the surface area. The skin is so thin that nutrients are absorbed from the water directly by the leaves.

## Swamp Plants

Swamp plants are adapted to changes in the water level caused by dry and rainy periods. Typical for this kind of plant is the *Nomaphila stricta*. These plants are able to grow beyond the water surface. The leaves that are in the air are much tougher than those under water. The plants nourish themselves mostly through the roots and only secondarily through the leaves.

◁ Upper left: Banded Barb *(Barbus semifasciolatus);*  Upper right: Two-Spot Barb *(Barbus ticto).* Middle left: Dwarf Rasbora *(Rasbora maculata);*  Middle right: Tiger or Sumatra Barb *(Barbus tetrazona).* Lower left: Island Barb *(Barbus oligalepis);*  Lower right: Black Ruby *(Barbus nigrofasciatus).*

# *Important Aquarium Plants*

**Aponogeton undulatus**

Light: bright.
Water: 68°–82°F
      (20°–28°C)
      pH 6.0–7.5
      dH 5–15
Some species shed leaves; new growth after 2–3 months.

**Cabomba caroliniana**

Light: very bright.
Water: 72°–82°F
      (22°–28°C)
      pH 6.5–7.2
      dH 12
Hardiest species of Cabomba; protect from debris and algae; needs $CO_2$ fertilizing.

**Ceratopteris thalicthroides**

Light: bright.
Water: 68°–82°F
      (20°–28°C)
      pH 6.5–7.5
      dH 3–12
Leave root crown exposed when planting; also floats.

**Cryptocoryne affinis**

Light: bright to to shady.
Water: 72°–82°F
      (22°–28°C)
      pH 6.0–7.5
      dH 3–15
Hardiest species; many others very sensitive; needs iron fertilizing.

**Echinodorus bleheri**

Light: bright to moderate shade.
Water: 72°–82°F
      (22°–28°C)
      pH 6.5–7.5
      dH 2–15
Species with lanceolate leaves should be planted singly; *Echinodorus tenellus* forms lawns.

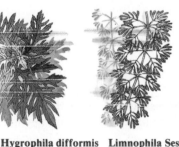

**Egeria (Elodea) densa**

Light: bright.
Water: 68°–79°F
      (20°–26°C)
      pH 6.5–7.5
      dH 8–18
Robust, fast-growing, produces $O_2$, cleans water. Good plant for beginners.

**Heteranthera zosterifolia**

Light: very bright.
Water: 72°–82°F
      (22°–28°C)
      pH 6.0–7.5
      dH 3–15
Grows fast when fertilized; used as thicket in background.

**Hygrophila polysperma**

Light; bright.
Water: 64°–86°F
      (18°–30°C)
      pH 6.5–7.5
      dH 3–15
Robust, undemanding, fast growing; good for beginners.

**Hygrophila difformis (Synnema triflorum)**

Light: very bright.
Water: 75°–82°F
      (24°–28°C)
      pH 6.5–7.5
      dH 2–15
Fast-growing when fertilized; good for beginners; loses leaves in insufficient light.

**Limnophila Sessiliflora**

Light: very bright.
Water: 72°–82°F
      (22°–28°C)
      pH 6.0–7.5
      dH 3–15
Needs iron fertilizing; renew periodically; protect from debris and algae.

# Important Aquarium Plants

   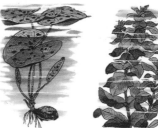 

**Microsorium pteropus**
Light: not too bright.
Water: 72°–82°F (22°–28°C) pH 5.5–7.0 dH 2–12
Tie to rocks, wood, or back wall; will form roots; rarely eaten by Cichlids.

**Myriophyllum aqua-ticum**
Light: bright.
Water: 72°–86°F (22°–30°–C) pH 5.0–7.5 dH 2–12
Favored for egg laying; protect from debris and algae.

**Nomaphila stricta (Hygrophila corym-bosa**
Light: bright.
Water: 72°–82°F (22°–28°C) pH 6.5–7.5 dH 4–15
Bright green or red; adaptable; fast growing; needs iron.

**Nymphaea lotus**
Light: bright to very
Water: 72°–82°F (22°–28°C) pH 5.5–7.5 dH 4–12
Green or red; if blossoms desired, leave floating leaves; fertilize frequently

**Rotala macrandra**
Light: very bright.
Water: 77°–86°F (25°–30°C) pH 6.0–7.5 dH 2–12
Red; good contrast with green plants; not for tanks with snails or robust, restless fish.

**Sagittaria subulata**
Light: bright to moderate shade.
Water: 72°–82°F (22°–28°C) pH 6.0–7.8 dH 3–17
Undemanding, fast-growing plant for beginners; multiplies through runners.

**Vallisneria spiralis**
Light: bright to very bright.
Water: 59°–86°F (15°–30°C) pH 6.5–7.5 dH 5–12
Undemanding, fast-growing plant for beginners; multiplies through runners.

**Vesicularia dubyana**
Light: bright to shady.
Water: 64°–86°F (18°–30°C) pH 5.8–7.5 dH 2–15
Undemanding; forms thick cushions, also grows on rocks and roots; used for egg laying.

**Pistia stratiotes**
Light: bright.
Water: 72°–77°F (22°–25°C) pH 6.5–7.2 dH 5–15
Should not be kept too warm; does not like water formed by condensation; therefore, do not keep tank tightly covered; floating plant.

**Riccia fluitans**
Light: bright.
Water: 59°–86°F (15°–30°C) pH 6.0–8.0 dH 5–15
Favored for egg laying; fast growing, forms thick cushions; floating plant.

# Aquarium Plants

## Plants in the Aquarium

Plants cannot establish a perfect biological equilibrium in the artificial environment of an aquarium, but they do contribute considerably to a healthy aquarium life. The fish like plants because they provide food, refuges, territorial borders, and spawning grounds. But the plants also improve the water quality by adding oxygen and absorbing harmful nitrogen compounds, and they keep the bottom material from rotting, because their roots give off oxygen. Luxuriant plants in an aquarium are not only a delight to the eye; they are also a biological necessity. It is well worth your while to take some care with them and create the conditions they need to flourish.

When you choose your plants, remember that they have to live in the same environment as the fish. Many *Cryptocoryne* species, as well as the *Cabomba aquatica,* do not thrive in hard water, while *Vallisneria spinalis* and *Elodea canadensis* do not grow in soft water. The latter two plants can be grown in a cold water tank, but the first two will die if they are kept in water below 68°F (20°C).

## Transport and Planting

The plants you buy at the store will be given to you in a plastic bag or wrapped in wet paper so that they will not dry out. When you get home, place them in a bowl and cover them with newspaper that will soak up water and keep the leaves that stick out of the water wet. While you fill the aquarium about one-third full with water you can disinfect the plants by placing them for ten minutes in a light purple solution of potassium permanganate or in water with 1 teaspoon of alum added per 1 quart (1 liter) of water. Remove all injured, wilted, or broken parts of the plant. Healthy roots are light in color and snap off when bent; dead ones are brown and limp. Take a sharp knife or scissors and trim the roots by one-third to one-half. This stimulates new growth. Do not bruise them.

When you are ready to plant, poke a hole in the bottom material, place the plant in it as deep as possible with the root tips pointing downward, fill the hole in, and press the sand gently around the plant. Now pull up the plant carefully until the crown of the root is just barely visible. This prevents the root tips from pointing upward, which makes it hard for the plant to take hold.

Plants of the *Echinodorus* genus and the *Aponogeton* genus have shallow root systems, and they are planted in oval-shaped hollows where the roots can be spread out. *Cryptocoryne* plants and *Valisneria spiralis,* whose roots grow straight down, should be planted in narrow, deep holes. Plants with creeping roots, such as the *Acorus* genus, should

# Aquarium Plants

be planted on a slant, so that the growth spots are not covered by sand. *Microsorium pteropus* and other ferns are placed just deep enough to still show their green root top. You can also tie these plants on to rocks, roots, or clay tiles, where they will set roots. Vine-forming plants like *Egeria* and *Cabomba* and *Nomaphila* sprout roots at the stem nodes. They are planted as cuttings after removing the lower leaf pairs. Hold them down with stones or glass clamps until they have grown roots.

## Plant Distribution

Plants are arranged for ornamental effect, but without crowding. The distance between plants depends on their size. Top-rooting plants should be spaced more widely than deep-rooting ones. The dealer will be able to advise you. For larger tanks it is best to make a diagram before you start planting. The largest plants belong in the back of the tank, while the front is either left bare or planted with a low ground cover. Of course, a magnificent large plant can be moved forward to catch the eye. The other plants are best arranged in small groups of the same kind rather than mixed all together. Red and brown plants show up nicely against green ones, as do light green plants against dark green ones.

If the aquarium receives more light at one end, that is where larger-growing plants should go. You can remove leaves infested with algae if necessary without its showing up too much. Also, fine-leafed plants that need a lot of light and are bothered by algae will do well in the vicinity of the large-growing plants.

## Fertilizing

Since tap water does not contain the nutrients and trace elements necessary for plant growth, you must supply them in the form of fertilizer. There are excellent liquid fertilizers, as well as tablets that are pressed into the bottom material near the plants. Swamp plants prefer the latter. How often you need to fertilize depends on the product you use. Fertilize only after you change the water. If you fertilize without changing the water, the plants will refuse to grow in spite of your best efforts. Fertilizers contain a number of different fertilizing salts, which the plants use up at different rates. If you keep adding fertilizer to the same water, some of these salts become highly concentrated, causing the plants to suffer and eventually die.

If you set up your aquarium primarily with the needs of plants in mind, you can place a long lasting, time-release fertilizer in the bottom gravel. At the same time you should install a heating cable so that

# Aquarium Plants

water will flow steadily through the bottom material (see page 16). Now all you need do is add some liquid fertilizer periodically. But in a tank like this you cannot keep burrowing fishes, including some Cichlids, Corydoras, and Loaches. Unfortunately, these are some of the most interesting fish for an aquarium.

For many plants, especially the *Cryptocoryne,* you must add iron to the water. (These plants usually do very well in tanks with slightly rusty metal frames.) Aquarists used to put a paper clip in the filter for this purpose, but now there are all-purpose fertilizers containing iron available. Iron fertilizing is definitely worthwhile in an aquarium with tropical plants.

But by far the most important plant nutrient is carbon dioxide. No matter how well you fertilize, if there is not enough $CO_2$ in the water, the plants will remain stunted. In the past, plant lovers would pour mineral water into the tank. If this was not overdone, the $CO_2$ did not lower the pH enough to harm the fish, but the mineral content would gradually build up. A much safer way to add the necessary $CO_2$ is to use pressurized bottles that are electronically controlled to give off steady small amounts of carbon dioxide. The technology involved is still being perfected, but the best products already on the market are quite safe and reliable.

## Plant Problems

Although plant diseases are rare in good water, light, and gravel, you should check your plants carefully from time to time.

New shoots and buds are, of course, a sign of health. Holes and dents in leaf edges in otherwise healthy plants are usually the result of nibbling. Both snails and fish like to chew off the ends of delicate plant leaves. It is another story altogether if plants refuse to grow or lose their color, or if their leaves become transparent or frayed. These are signs of ill health due to over- or under-feeding.

• If all the plant leaves turn completely yellow and then glassy, this is a sign of *iron deficiency.* It can be corrected by the addition of iron or a complete fertilizer.

• Yellow leaves with green veins indicate a deficiency in trace elements, especially *manganese.* This can develop from overfeeding with iron alone instead of feeding with complete fertilizers.

• Brown and black discoloration with subsequent decaying of the leaves is also caused by overfeeding with iron.

• As pointed out before, carbon dioxide is the most important plant nutrient. Some plants, especially those that normally occur in hard water, are able to draw $CO_2$ out of the water and use it for biosynthetic decalcification; others that live in soft water cannot do this. That is why you cannot keep plants from soft

# *Aquarium Plants*

water and plants from hard water in the same tank without adding $CO_2$. Biosynthetic decalcification can raise the pH of the water so high (to 9 or 10) that plants used to soft or slightly acid water suffer and fish may die of alkaline toxicity.

• The most dreaded plant disease is *Cryptocoryne* rot. First, there are holes in the leaves that look as though they had been caused by nibbling fish. But within a few days, the plants can collapse and rot. The disease is probably caused by excess nitrates. Tap water contains a lot of nitrates that do not occur in natural water, and fish excreta as well as food debris keep adding nitrates to the water in the tank. Plants that naturally grow in water high in nitrates can break them down into ammonium, which they feed on; but other plants, such as the *Cryptocoryne,* that live in water with plenty of ammonium cannot do this. These plants take up the nitrates and store them. When there is a sudden change in the environment, the nitrates are transformed into toxic nitrogen compounds that can kill the plants. Such a sudden change occurs after a long overdue change of water, the replacement of an old, worn-out fluorescent tube, or after the infrequent addition of fertilizer.

Plant problems can easily be prevented
• if the plants are kept in a constant environment;
• if the nitrate content is kept low by regular water changes;
• if a well-balanced fertilizer is added after the water is changed, providing the plants with the nutrients they need but no more;
• if fluorescent tubes are replaced regularly so that plants are not subjected to abrupt changes in lighting.

## Algae

Algae are simple water plants whose spores are introduced into the tank by water, fish, plant food, and/or live fish food. There are always some algae present in an aquarium. As long as conditions are favorable for the plants (i.e., bottom gravel and water are in good shape and there is a proper amount of fertilizer), rivals will not thrive. Strong, sturdy plants improve water so much that algae do not have a chance. But as soon as environmental factors start acting negatively on plants, the water tends to deteriorate; and algae, which do not need the same water quality as plants, will multiply very rapidly. The following kinds of algae are found in aquariums:

• *Blue-green algae* are the oldest form of algae and are the greatest nuisance. They form a dense blue-green, violet, or brownish-black layer on the bottom, on rocks, and on plants. You can strip these slimy algae off by hand or siphon them off. But they will grow back if even a trace of them is left in the tank. Unfor-

tunately, no aquarium dwellers eat them.
• *Red algae* grow in dirty-green threads or beards from plants, wood, and rocks. They are just as persistent as blue-green algae. Some aquarium fishes (e.g., the Siamese Flying Fox *(Epalzeorhynchus siamensis)* enjoy feeding on them.
• *Brown algae* and gravel algae usually grow in a thin brown layer on ornamental and other objects as well as on plants. Their presence indicates inadequate light and oxygen. If stronger light is provided, they soon disappear again, since plants assimilate nutrients and produce oxygen more efficiently in brighter light.
• *Green algae* seldom occur in great quantities. Light green floating algae turn aquarium water into an opaque green brew. Sometimes green algae appear in newly set up aquariums where the fish are overfed. They vanish when light is reduced for a few days, or if a large number of water fleas are introduced into the tank. (Be sure and stop your filter.) Afterwards, the fattened water fleas can be fed to the fish. Other kinds of green algae form in a lush, green, cottonlike growth. They can be removed either by hand or siphoned off. Green thread-like algae grow only in clean, well fertilized aquariums where everything is as it should be. Their presence is, then, a good sign. Unfortunately, they form webs around water plants and thus deprive them of light. Fine-leafed plants needing bright light

can be choked to death by this type of algae. If you remove the algae by hand, be careful not to pull up the plants.

Some fishes like to eat algae (see page 22), but if the algae grow so fast that neither the fish nor you can keep ahead of them, you may need to use a chemical killer. Use these products strictly according to instructions, since higher concentrations will cause other water plants to die.

Important: The easiest way to prevent algae infestations is to place enough plants in the aquarium at the very beginning. Many aquarists spare no money on tank and equipment and then skimp on plants. In a sparsely planted tank, algae thrive. If you start out with lots of inexpensive but healthy plants, you can thin them after a few months and replace them gradually with more demanding and expensive ones. Algae will not become a problem at that time.

## Snails in an Aquarium

Every community aquarium has snails which consume leftover food that the fish refuse to eat. You hardly ever have to purchase these scavengers because there are usually some snail eggs on the aquarium plants, or they may get into the tank with the live food. Three kinds of snails do well in a warm-water aquarium:
• Ramshorn snails *(Planorbis corneus)*

are found most often in aquariums. They hardly ever damage plants unless they are present in large numbers. Only finely leafed aquarium plants like the *Cabomba aquatica* are sometimes subject to their attacks.

• Malayan snails *(Melanoides tuberculata)* live and burrow in the bottom gravel. These snails are livebearers. During the day, they stay underground; they emerge only at night. They rarely eat plants. Their constant digging and burrowing causes debris to get into the bottom gravel, where it is more available to the plants but also contributes to the rotting of the bottom material.

• The South American snails of the genus *Ampullaris* can grow to almost the size of escargots. These snails are seldom available in pet stores. They eat fish food and plants, but if there is enough other food, they rarely harm living plants.

Occasionally mud snails *(Limnaea stagnalis)* are introduced into an aquarium with the live food. These snails feed on plants and may carry diseases. They are difficult to get rid of.

If the snails threaten to take over, you should not automatically reach for a snail pesticide, because these chemicals also harm sensitive fishes. Try placing a scalded lettuce leaf in the aquarium overnight. Lots of snails will collect on it. By doing this once a week or once a month, you can probably hold the snail population in check. Also, Puffer Fish and large Cichlids like to eat the snails that you collect.

Important: The behavior of the snails is an excellent indicator of the water quality in the tank. If they move around actively on the bottom and on the plants and eat a clear trail through the algae on the glass, there is nothing wrong with the water. But if they lie around lethargically, there are some toxic substances in the water (products of nitrogen decomposition, heavy metals, harmful synthetic materials). If the Malayan snails remain on the surface during the day instead of burrowing, this means that the bottom material is rotting. If a great number of snails die off within a short period, it is high time for a thorough chemical analysis of the aquarium water.

47

# Selection and Care of Fishes

## Description of the Most Common Species

### Characins *(Characoidei)*

**Geographical origin:** Tropical and subtropical America, also Africa. **Habitat:** Flowing and still waters. **Distinguishing feature:** Most have adipose fins. **Characteristics:** Most Characins (Tetras and their relatives) travel in schools. Their bright colors aid recognition of members of species and serve to keep the school together. The breeds with luminous markings, such as the Neon Tetra *(Paracheirodon innesi)* and the Glowlight Tetra *(Hemigrammus erythrozonus)* come from rivers with clear and black water, while light-colored and silvery Characins, like the Rummy-Nose Tetra *(Hemigrammus rhodostomus),* occur naturally in flat-land creeks and rivers carrying white and clear water.

**Aquarium care:** Almost all Tetras and their relatives are suitable for community aquariums as long as they do not get too big. The most widely favored breeds belong to the genera *Hyphessobrycon, Hemigrammus, Cheirodon,* and *Aphyocharax.* However, Hatchetfish *(Gasteropelecidae)* should be combined only with peaceful bottom dwellers. Hatchetfish need long, well-covered tanks because, with their huge pectoral fins, they can leap through the air as far as nine to fifteen feet (3–5 m). They are very sensitive to polluted water and should be fed only live food. Ornamental Characins of the genera *Nannostomus* and *Poecilobrycon* should not be kept with large, fast-swimming species. They need a dense growth of plants, as well as floating plants, and with their tiny mouths they can eat only finely minced food. Piranhas *(Serrasalmidae)* also do not belong in a community aquarium. While it is possible to keep Piranhas that grow to more than 1 foot (30 cm), such as the Red-Bellied Piranha *(Serrasalmus nattereri),* in an aquarium, they endanger not only fish of other species but also each other. They are too sensitive to stress and need clean, frequently renewed water. Other genera belonging to this family are *Mylossoma, Metynnis,* and *Myloplus.* Piranhas feed only on fresh lettuce and water plants, and they need tanks at least 60 inches (150 cm) long to grow to full size. They are sensitive and easily frightened. Large predatory Characins like the Bucktoothed Tetra *(Exodon paradoxus)* indicate by their appearance alone that they do not belong in a community aquarium. Some Headstanders of the *Leporinus* and *Anostomus* species are very aggressive, eat plants, and are not suitable for a community aquarium either.

If you buy Characins, never get just "a couple" of one species but always at least seven to ten. These fish are so small that you can keep them in a tank as small as 20 inches (50 cm) long. A larger tank shows off schools of them much better, of course. These fish need a large swimming area in the middle of the tank and dense plant growth around the edges to hide in when they are pursued.

**Water:** Soft to medium hard, slightly acid; breeds originating in mixed black and clear water need peat-filtered water. **Temperature:** 72–79°F (22°–26°C).**Food:** Dry food, small-sized live food.

### Barbs and Other Cyprinids *(Cyprinoidei)*

**Geographical Origin:** Worldwide except for South America and Australia. Genera suitable for aquariums are: *Puntius* (Barbs), *Rasbora, Danio, Brachydanio,* and *Labeo.* Most of these come from India and Southeast Asia, some from Africa. **Habitat:** Fairly fast-moving water. **Distinguishing feature:** Most have one or two barbels at the corners of the mouth. **Characteristics:** Swim in schools; persistent swimmers; many species are bottom feeders.

**Aquarium care:** Most Cyprinids need large tanks with a large swimming area, hiding places, and perhaps a loose network of floating plants that shades some of the tank. They should not be combined with very peaceful, shy fishes. *Rasbora* species jump and should therefore be in a well-covered tank. The *Labeo* species (also called Sharks) are interesting fish to keep but need large tanks. They resemble Loaches in body shape and aquarium needs (see below). *Labeos,* especially the Red-Tailed Shark *(Labeo bicolor),* establish ranking orders. The top-ranking fish has the most intensive coloring and will in too small a tank terrorize all the others. You therefore have to supply enough refuges if you want to keep a group of Red-Tailed Sharks. The males of the Giant Danio *(Danio aequipinnatus)* also form ranking orders. The Tiger or Sumatra Barb *(Barbus tetrazona)* and its relatives are not suited for community tanks because they nip off the long fins of other fishes (e.g., Angelfish). They even go after the long barbels of Corydoras. The Bala Shark *(Balantiocheilos melanopterus)* and other large, plant-eating Barb species should also be kept out of a group aquarium. Bottom feeders need an especially effective filtering system in the tank. And do not try to grow finely leafed plants. **Water:** Soft to medium hard, slightly acid; some species need peat filtering. **Temperature:** 73°–79°F (23°–26°C). **Food:** Dry and live foods of all kinds. *Labeos* are mostly herbivorous.

## Loaches *(Cobitidae)*
## Algae-Eaters *(Gyrinocheilidae)*

**Geographical origin:** Europe and Asia; species for aquarium use: Southeast Asia. **Habitat:** Still and moving waters. **Distinguishing features:** Body shape typical of bottom feeders; at least three pairs of barbels; and a moveable spine near each eye that is raised at any sign of danger. **Characteristics:** Loaches have an intestinal "lung." If they are forced to live in water that is low in oxygen, they rise to the surface, where they swallow air and release it through the anal opening. Very little is known about how they live in their natural habitat. Some loaches form schools when they are still young. If they are kept singly when young, they usually waste away. The adults of some species are territorial and often extremely aggressive.

**Aquarium care:** Loaches are usually shy and need a large, quiet tank with lots of hiding places and not too much light. The bottom material should be soft and of fine sand since these fish constantly burrow for food with their barbels. Hiding places can be provided in the form of wood, piles of flagstones, and coconut shells. The more nooks and crannies there are to hide in, the less shy these fish are. The Dwarf Loaches *(Botia sidthimunki)* live in schools and are continually on the move. They are the only species of Loaches that prefer the middle range of the tank. The wormlike Loaches of the genus *Acanthophthalmus* like to burrow completely into the bottom material. Dwarf Loaches are the only ones that are suitable for group aquariums. All the others are too large and too shy. **Water:** Soft to medium hard, slightly acid; some Loaches should have peat filtering. **Temperature:** 77°–82°F (25°–28°C). **Food:** Live food of all kinds, especially worms; also dry foods.

The Algae-Eater *(Gyrinocheilus aymonieri),* usually sold as the Chinese Algae-Eater, comes from the fast waters of rivers in Southeast Asia. It has a wide, overshot mouth with strong lips that enable it to cling to rocks so that it will not be carried along even in strong currents. The mouth also serves to clean off algae at an amazing rate. When young, the Algae-Eater is a peaceful fish, feeding entirely on algae, but as it gets older, it acquires territorial habits and becomes partially carnivorous. It likes well aerated water since it is used to fast currents.
**Water:** Soft to medium hard. **Temperature:** 72°–79°F (22°–26°C). **Food:** Algae, spinach, dry foods from plant and animal sources.

## Catfishes *(Siluroidei)*

**Geographical origin:** Worldwide, mainly in fresh water, some in salt water. **Habitat:** Still and moving waters, frequents undercut banks. **Distinguishing features:** Barbels with sensory cells for taste and touch; usually adipose fins; no scales; naked skin, or armored with bony plates. **Characteristics:** Most Catfishes are bottom dwellers and active at night. They have small eyes but well-developed barbels. Fish that are active at dusk and orient themselves by vision have normal-size or enlarged eyes. Some Catfishes, like the Glass Catfish *(Kryptopterus bicirrhis)* and the *Corydoras hastatus,* are active during the day and swim around constantly, while others dig themselves into the ground during the day (e.g., *Bunocephalus kneri).* There are large and small Armored Catfishes *(Loricariidae)* that live mostly on algae. The Albino Clarias *(Clarias batrachus)* and other meat-eaters should be kept together only with robust fishes of similar size. The Albino Clarias have accessory breathing organs that allow them to breathe outside the water. They can even migrate from a lake that has dried up to another one with water. The Electric Catfish *(Malapterurus electricus)* from tropical Africa has electric organs, made up of electroplates that are derived from muscle cells, capable of emitting electric currents of up to 400 volts with which they stun enemies and prey. Many Catfishes hatch their eggs, and some marine species are mouth-breeders. Our aquariums house primarily Thorny Catfishes *(Doradidae),* Upside-down Catfishes *(Mochokidae),* Mailed Catfishes *(Callichthyidae),* and Armored Catfishes *(Loricariidae).* Thorny Catfishes grow to more than 6 inches (15 cm) and should be kept only in large tanks. If you lift a Thorny Catfish out of the water, it can quack and complain and even growl by moving its extended pectoral spiny fins back and forth in the shoulder joints.

The African Upside-Down Catfishes have feathered barbels on their lower jaws. They live in groups. The Black-Bellied Upside-Down Catfish *(Synodontis nigriventris)* from the Congo basin belongs to this family. It swims on its back and eats in that position. During the day it hides under roots or leaves. In this species the belly is darker than the back as a result of adaptation to this unusual swimming position. When they are first hatched, these fish swim normally.

The South American Mailed Catfishes *(Callichthyidae)* are the most common Catfishes in our aquariums, especially members of the genus *Corydoras.* These are the "typical" aquarium Catfish. Their whole bodies are covered with bony plates. Like the Loaches, they have intestinal breathing organs because they are used to shallow shore water that is low in oxygen. Catfishes with armored plates, such as the Peppered Corydoras *(Corydoras paleatus),* often deposit eggs even in a community aquarium. The Armored Catfishes also originate in South America. They live in very fast streams and have developed an overshot sucker mouth with which they mow off algae. During the spawning season the males of many species develop skin protrusions on the head that look like dense bristles or beards. Armored Catfishes are herbivorous and cannot live solely on food from animal sources. They are some of the most effective algae cleaners in our aquariums.

**Aquarium care:** Catfishes need refuges where they can hide during the day. Bottom feeders

should have soft sand. These fishes are ideal for people who work during the day. The fish only start getting active when you get home from work. All Armored Catfishes, as well as the smaller Upside-Down Catfishes, do well in a group aquarium. But Catfishes with broad sucker mouths and well-developed barbels are usually good hunters, and a whole school of lovely bright Tetras may disappear overnight. The most dangerous hunters belong to the larger species of the *Clarias* and *Heteropneustes* genera. But some members of the *Bagridae* family, such as the Barred Siamese Catfish *(Leiocassis Siamensis),* may present too much of a risk to a community aquarium as adults.

**Water:** Soft to medium hard, slightly acid; peat filtering necessary for breeds from black and clear waters. **Temperature:** 72°–80°F (22°–27°C), depending on place of origin. **Food:** Live and dry food of all kinds, especially worms and mosquito larvae.

## Egg-laying Toothed Carps *(Cyprinodontidae)*

**Geographical origin:** Tropical and subtropical parts of the New and Old Worlds. **Habitat:** Still and moving waters; rain puddles. **Distinguishing features:** Body shape of surface-water fishes; males brightly colored; females duller and smaller. **Characteristics:** The reproductive mechanism of some African and South American species is one of the strangest we know. These fishes live in small puddles of rain water that dry up in the hot season. The fish spawn here and press their eggs into the ground. During the dry season the puddles dry up, and all the fish die, but the eggs survive in the mud. As soon as it rains, the eggs hatch, and within a few months the young develop into adults who spawn at the end of the rain season. These Killifish are called "annual" because the whole life cycle from birth to spawning to death occurs within one year. There are also species that are not annual and live in permanent water where they deposit their eggs on the bottom or on plants.

**Aquarium care:** Many of the approximately 430 species of Killifishes can be bred by the hobbyist as long as the conditions under which the eggs normally develop are carefully observed. But these fish are very fussy about water quality and should be kept in a tank by themselves.

# Selection and Care of Fishes

**Water:** Very soft to medium hard, depending on the species; some need sea salt added to the water, and some require peat filtering. **Temperature:** 64°–72°F (18°–22°C), somewhat higher for breeding. **Food:** Live food, especially insects and mosquito larvae; also dry food.

Consult specialized literature for individual species.

### Live-bearing Toothed Carps *(Poeciliidae)*

**Geographical origin:** Americas (southern U.S. to northern Argentina); imported to control mosquitoes in many countries. **Habitat:** Slow-moving streams, still water; also along the coast. **Distinguishing features:** Body type of surface-water fishes; males more colorful than females; females larger than males. **Characteristics:** The anal fin of the male is modified into an organ of copulation called the gonopodium. When mating, the male inserts this into the female; some of the sperm fertilizes the eggs, while the rest is deposited and stored in the folds of the ovarian tubes. This way successive batches of eggs can be fertilized without the male being present. The young grow inside the female and break out of the eggs at the time of birth. This system protects the young from predators and other dangers they would be exposed to in the water. One species from the Amazon *(Poecilia formosa)* has exclusively females. These mate with males of other species. The sperm dies in the egg after having stimulated the development of the egg, but the fry are all female. It used to be thought that the Swordtails *(Xiphophorus helleri)* underwent a sex change because "old" females seemed to turn into fertile males "according to need." But it turned out that in this species there are two forms of males, "early" and "late" ones, and the late male resembles the female in appearance.

**Aquarium care:** Live-bearing Toothed Carps are hardy and undemanding. Breeding them is so easy that even beginners will enjoy it. Live-bearers are ideal for anyone setting up a first aquarium. But although they are unproblematic, they should be tended with the same care as other fishes. Small species need only small tanks, but Swordtails and other large-finned types need tanks at least 40 inches (100 cm) long. Provide ample swimming space with plants only around the edges for species that like to swim. A loose cover of floating plants is good for these fishes because in nature, too, they dwell among such plants. The bottom material should be dark in color.

**Water:** Medium hard to hard; neutral to slightly alkaline. Some Mollies from coastal areas, such as the Sailfin Molly *(Poecilia latipinna),* the Sphenops Molly *(Poecilia sphenops),* and the Yucatan Sailfin Molly *(Poecilia velifera),* need some sea salt in the water. **Temperature:** Depends on the place of origin. Guppies *(Poecilia reticulata)* 64°–73°F (18°–23°C); Platies *(Xiphophorus maculatus)* 68°–77°F (20°–25°C); Swordtails *(Xiphophorus helleri)* 68°–77°F (20°–25°C); Yucatan Sailfin Mollies *(Poecilia velifera)* 73°–82°F (23°–28°C). **Food:** Dry and live foods of all sorts, especially mosquito larvae and insects. Also plants, especially for fishes that live near the coast. **Breeds:** There are many ornamental breeds of live-bearing Toothed Carps. Selective breeding has produced Guppies with fins of all shapes and colors, Platies in many color variations, and Swordtails with variously shaped and colored fins and different overall colorations. All the strains within a species can be crossed, as can some members of different species. If you have live-bearers in a community aquarium, you should therefore restrict yourself to one species or a specific strain of one species. It is practically impossible to keep live-bearers from breeding, and random crosses are not popular with dealers or even hobbyists. And it is sad to have to sell the offspring as fish food.

If the wild form of a species is kept together with an ornamental one, successive offspring will revert more and more to the wild form. The highly bred, large-finned males move much more slowly than the wild males who thus reach the females first.

Anyone wanting to breed live-bearing Toothed Carps should be sure to get females that have not previously been with males. Pregnant females have a dark pregnancy mark in front of the anal fin. Even very young females are capable of mating; and, since one fertilization is sufficient for a number of egg batches, she may unexpectedly produce mixed breeds of unknown origin. Even the young of your own production must be segregated by sex as soon as the sex can be recognized. All cultivated strains need higher temperatures and are more demanding in the quality of the water than wild forms.

# Selection and Care of Fishes

**Silversides** *(Atherinidae)*

**Geographical origin:** Madagascar, Australia.
**Characteristics:** The species most frequently found in the tanks of dealers belong to the genus *Melanotaenia* (Rainbow Fish). All of them are lively and undemanding and live in schools. **Water:** Medium hard to hard, possibly with a little sea salt. **Temperature:** 72°–79°F (22°–26°C). **Food:** Dry and live food of all kinds.

**Cichlids** *(Cichlidae)*

**Geographical origin:** South and Central America, Africa, India. **Habitat:** Most Cichlids live along the shores of lakes and rivers, preferably where the bank is undercut beneath roots and rocks and there are plenty of spots to hide in. Some species live near the rocky shores of fresh-water lakes. Cichlids are rarely found where there are only sand and rocks without vegetation. **Distinguishing feature:** The dorsal fin is hard at the front and has soft rays at the back. **Characteristics:** All Cichlids look after their eggs and young. This behavior takes the following forms:

*Open breeding:* These fishes deposit their camouflage-colored eggs on rocks or leaves. Males and females look alike. A pair will form a bond that lasts beyond the spawning period. Both partners participate in the courtship ritual and defend their territory, clean a spawning place, and look after the eggs and fry together. Angelfish *(Pterophyllum scalare)*, Convict Cichlids *(Cichlasoma nigrofasciatum)*, Jewel Cichlids *(Hemichromis bimaculatus)*, Red Discus *(Symphysodon discus)* and Orange Chromides *(Etroplus maculatus)* nurse their young during the first few days after hatching with a secretion from the skin.

*Protected breeding:* These fishes lay larger eggs than the open breeders. Some species deposit their eggs in caves; others carry them in their mouths until the young are old enough to survive without protection. The males are mostly much larger and more colorful than the females, which resemble their surroundings in color. Many pairs stay together only for one mating season or even just for the hatching of one batch of eggs. Usually the female looks after the eggs by herself.

The protected breeding behavior can be further divided into:

*Cave breeding:* Often several female cave-breeders live and mate with one male in a territory. The spawning takes place in caves. The male leaves the care of the eggs and fry to the females but protects the territory. In some species, e.g., the Lyretail Lamprologus *(Lamprologus brichardi)* and the Dwarf Cichlids of the genus *Julidochromis* from Lake Tanganyika, the young from earlier spawnings help raise the new fry and defend the territory.

*Mouth breeding:* Mouthbreeders typically stay together only for spawning. The males live in colonies, never alone. They build nursery pits and court each passing female. If she is ready to spawn, she follows the male, deposits a few eggs in the pit, and then takes them into her mouth. The eggs are fertilized in the sand or in the mouth of the female. The males of some African mouthbreeders, like Burton's Mouthbrooder *(Haplochromis burtoni),* have spots or marks on their anal fins that look like eggs and that attract the female to the male's vent, where she picks up sperm. Usually a female moves from one male to another in the course of spawning. The young hatch in the mother's mouth and return there in moments of danger even after they have been swimming free.

**Aquarium care:** Apart from the Angelfish, few of this family can share a typical community tank containing members of the Characidae and Cyprinidae families. They need to be in a tank of their own. One possible combination is a Golden Dwarf Cichlid *(Nannacara anomala)* together with a Kribensis *(Pelvicachromis pulcher)*. Cichlids are territorial and aggressive even against members of their own genus. They need hiding places and caves for spawning and are quite capable of rearranging the whole aquarium according to their own needs. Since their needs seldom coincide with the hobbyist's desires, these fishes have acquired a reputation as ruffians that "turn the whole aquarium upside down." If they do dig up everything in your tank, it is a sure sign that it is too small or improperly planned for them. To be able to witness their fascinating mating behavior, you should give them a tank 30 inches (80 cm) long, or more. Even the smaller breeds need a lot of space because of their interesting social systems.

# Selection and Care of Fishes

Adult Cichlids are aggressive toward each other. If several males and females live together, there will soon be a definite ranking order. The largest fish dominates the whole tank and chases everyone in it. The second largest chases everyone smaller than he, and so on. The smallest fish may be chased to death. Even contests between evenly matched rivals for territory or females can end in death.

Open breeders should be kept in pairs. In the case of cave breeding, one male can have a harem of females. The same is recommended for mouth-breeders because males will court to death a female that is not ready to spawn. A male's aggressive energies are more safely used up in the presence of several females.

Newcomers in a tank of Cichlids are, of course, in special danger. They find themselves in an environment where all the territories are occupied and there is no chance to get away. An aquarium with Cichlids should therefore have a number of fair-sized rock structures in which the smaller fish can hide. You can also place robust plants in the tank. If they are located at the territorial borders, they will probably not be dug up because Cichlids usually choose spawning spots in the center of the tank. A loose network of floating plants is desirable for many species.

**Water:** South and Central American species of the genera *Aequidens, Astronotus, Cichlasoma, Geophagus, Herichthys,* and *Pterophyllum,* as well as Dwarf Cichlids of the *Apistogramma* and *Papiliochromis* genera, require soft and slightly acid water, as do species from West and Central Africa of the genera *Lamprologus, Pelmatochromis, Pelvicachromis, Sarotherodon, Steatocranus,* and *Tilapia.* The *Pelvicachromis* may need some sea salt. The genera *Haplochromis, Julidochromis, Labeotropheus, Labidochromis, Lamprologus, Melanochromis, Pseudotropheus, Tropheus,* and others from the East African lakes need medium hard to hard and alkaline water. Indian species like *Etroplus maculatus* and *Etroplus suratensis* live in brackish water. **Temperature:** 72°-79°F (22°-26°C) depending on origin, 82°F (28°C) for breeding. **Food:** Dry and live food of all kinds and suitable to the size of the fish. Some species, especially the Cichlids from Lakes Malawi and Tanganyika need vegetarian food.

Consult specialized literature on the requirements for individual species.

## Labyrinth Fishes *(Anabantoidei)*

**Geographical origin:** Southeast Asia, Africa. **Habitat:** Shallow, overgrown waters; irrigation channels; and flooded rice fields that warm up to and above 86°F (30°C). **Distinguishing feature:** Labyrinth Fishes (Anabantoids) have an auxiliary breathing organ, the so-called labyrinth, with which they can absorb air. This labyrinth is located in the upper part of the gill cavity. The air is taken in through the mouth and pushed into the labyrinth. Labyrinth fishes that are prevented from taking in air will drown. **Characteristics:** Because of their ability to breathe air, a result of adaptation to their environment, Labyrinth Fish survive even in badly polluted water with very little oxygen. The males of several species build bubble nests among plant leaves, e.g., the Siamese Fighting Fish *(Betta splendens),* the Paradise Fish *(Macropodus opercularis)* and the Gouramis (genera *Trichogaster* and *Colisa).* The fish takes up air in its mouth, coats it with saliva, and spits the bubbles, which stick together, to the surface of the water. Some species like the Dwarf Gourami *(Colisa lalia)* incorporate plant materials in their bubble nests. Only the males build nests and take care of the eggs and young. The fish spawn under the nest, and the eggs float upward. Eggs that float downward are caught by the male who spits them back into the nest. After spawning has occurred, he chases away the female, defends the nest, and keeps spitting eggs and fry back into the nest if they fall out. He does this until the fry are ready to swim on their own.

There are also mouth-breeding Labyrinth fishes, and among the Chocolate Gouramis *(Sphaerichthys osphromenoides),* both mouthbreeding and bubble-nest building occurs. The mouthbreeders live in fast water, the bubble nest builders in still water.

**Aquarium care:** The magnificently colored males of the Labyrinth Fishes do not get along well with each other. The worst fighters are the Siamese Fighting Fish *(Betta splendens),* the Paradise Fish *(Macropodus),* and the African *Ctenopoma.* These even bite the females to death if they are not yet

# Selection and Care of Fishes

ready to spawn or are past spawning. You can keep more than one of these males only in a very large aquarium. They have to have enough space to form territories. Many Labyrinth Fishes are easy to keep. Among these are the genera *Betta* and *Macropodus* and the robust Gouramis of the genera *Trichogaster* and *Colisa*. Even beginners will have no trouble breeding these in a group aquarium, though the larger fish will eat the young. A tank with Labyrinth Fishes should be densely planted and well lighted. Floating plants will facilitate nest building.

**Water:** Soft to medium hard; most species are not fussy about water quality. Only the Mosaic Gourami *(Trichogaster leeri)* and the *Trichopsis schalleri* need soft, slightly acid water. **Temperature:** 73°–81°F (23°–27°C); 86°F (30°C) for breeding. **Food:** Dry and live foods of all sorts suitable to the size of the fish. African *Ctenopoma* will also feed on small fish.

## What to Watch Out for When You Buy Fish

If you have followed the advice of this book so far, you will have a fair idea of what fishes will populate your aquarium. You will have chosen fishes that require the same or similar types of water, that will not fight or get in each other's way, and that will populate the different water strata. Taking all this into account, you will have come up with a collection that will make for an attractive, colorful aquarium. Most of the species we have mentioned in our survey of aquarium fishes are available in pet stores. The sales person will be happy to assist you with advice. A knowledgeable dealer knows not only the names of all the fishes he sells but also what each species should be fed and how it should be kept. But if you buy your fish in a large department store, you should be cautious. There the sales personnel are usually ill-equipped to answer specialized questions. In case of doubt, ask for the manager of the pet department who will have the necessary expertise.

The fish that you buy should not have any small white spots or fuzzy white deposits on the body; their fins should not be fringed; and their skin should not look cloudy. They should be well-fed but not bloated. They should swim actively but not dart nervously, and they should not be emaciated and remain motionless in a corner. Do not ever buy fish from an aquarium where the water looks yellowish or a fluorescent green or blue. Such discolorations are the result of medications and indicate that the fish in the tank are sick.

## Transport and Acclimatization

Fish are usually packed in plastic bags for taking home. That will do for short trips. For longer ones (24 hours or more) pure oxygen should be pumped into the bag. Spiny fishes may puncture plastic bags with their sharp fins. They should be carried in double bags, or better, in Mason jars or small buckets. (Take these with you when you go to buy fish.) In cold, winter weather the container should be wrapped in newspaper or, better, placed in a styrofoam box.

When you get home with your fish, open the bag and hang it in your tank. You can hold it in place with the cover, or you can clamp it to the glass with a clothespin so that it will not tip over. Now add aquarium water to the bag by drops or dribbles until the water temperature is the same in the bag and the tank and the fish are adjusted to the water conditions. After you have added about as much aquarium water as was originally in the bag, you can turn the bag upside down and release the fish into the tank. If you do not want water from the pet store in your tank, you can take the fish out of the bag with a net. Or you

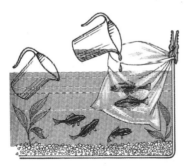

The right way to transfer fish to your tank: The plastic bag is opened, hung inside the tank, and slowly filled with water from the tank.

can pour the water from the bag into a bucket and then add aquarium water as described above. You can place an air-stone in the bucket to supply extra oxygen. If you have a quarantine tank, you should keep new fish in it for a few days to see if there are any signs of disease. Fish that look healthy at the dealer's may be overtaxed by the trip home, and a latent disease may break out. That is why you should not buy new fish before you go off on a vacation. If you do, the person looking after your fish may be faced with unpleasant surprises.

As a conscientious aquarist, you will probably go to the pet store once a week to get fresh food for your fish, and you should certainly go at least once a month to replace filter materials. Every time you go you will be tempted by a huge array of beautiful fishes from all over the world, and you will have to learn to resist the desire to buy "just one more." You cannot keep adding new fish, no matter how beautiful they are. The space in any tank is limited. Frequently the hand-somest fishes you see are incompatible with the ones you already have. Some-times you will see newly imported fishes about which even the dealer is not knowl-edgeable. You should stay away from these, unless you happen to have a newly set up and still unpopulated tank waiting. Do not buy unfamiliar fishes on the spur of the moment.

# Selection and Care of Fishes

## The Diseases of Fishes

If you observe the requirements of the species you have and keep the water in good shape, you should not have any trouble with diseases. The only thing that may happen is that some parasitic disease may be introduced by fungi or protozoans on plants, new fish, or live food. Parasites are usually easy to recognize and can be quickly and effectively treated with medications available at pet stores. But treatment must be initiated as soon as the parasites are discovered. If parasites like *Ichthyophthirius multifiliis* have time to spread, they can do serious harm and are hard to combat. Diseases are caused not only by plant and animal parasites but also by bacteria and viruses. Most of these are present in any aquarium without ill effects on the fish. They attack only fish whose resistance is lowered by an inappropriate environment, such as an overcrowded, poorly aerated and filtered tank. The weakest fish are the first to get ill, and they infect the others. Under especially unfavorable conditions the entire population of a tank can die off within a few days. Most diseases can be prevented if you follow just a few important rules:
• An aquarium should house only fishes with similar water requirements and that do not attack each other.
• The tank should not be overcrowded (1½ to 2 quarts [1½–2 liters] of water per ½ inch [1 cm] of fish length).
• The tank has to have an effective filter that is cleaned out regularly. If the aquarium is longer than 30 inches (80 cm), it should be aerated with a water pump, because most parasites and disease-carrying agents do not thrive in agitated water.
• Newly purchased fish should be placed in a quarantine tank for three to seven days.

The most common and serious internal disease fish are subject to is *tuberculosis.* (Fish tuberculosis is not contagious to humans.) About 80% of all aquarium fish are permanently infected with TB. This disease spreads fastest in an overpopulated aquarium. For this reason, you should not combine livebearing Toothed Carps from brackish water with Scalares and Discus Fish from areas with acid, low-mineral black water or with Loaches from fast-moving mountain streams. As long as the water in a tank with such a combination of fish is clean and the food nutritious, none of the fish will be really ill, but none will thrive either. Then, if the water deteriorates for some reason, tuberculosis breaks out. Once the fish are weakened by TB, they become more subject to other infections and attacks by parasites. Effective medication against tuberculosis has not yet been developed, but it usually suffices if additional infections are warded off and environmental conditions improved.

# Selection and Care of Fishes

Not only diseases but also negligence on the part of the hobbyist can do serious harm. You should check the pH of the water regularly. Water that is too acid or alkaline damages the gills and skin. The water can be poisoned by water softeners, chemicals, or heavy metals. If a poorly covered aquarium is kept in a room where people smoke a lot, fish can die of nicotine poisoning. Insecticides should not be used near an aquarium. Even insecticides with a pyrethrum base that are not harmful to other animals are toxic for fish.

Further symptoms of the most common fish diseases are:

**Clamped fins and rocking of body:** A sign of general ill-health; initial stages of internal or parasitic diseases; water too cold.

**Lack of appetite:** Intestinal diseases; *Ichthyosporidium;* tuberculosis.

**Resting on the bottom:** Swim-bladder disease; tuberculosis.

**Reeling, headstanding:** Usually *Ichthyosporidium* or tuberculosis.

**Gasping for air:** Gill parasites; lack of oxygen; ammonia or nitrite poisoning; gill rot.

**Rubbing against objects:** Ectoparasites; acid or alkaline toxicity.

**Fast darting around:** Parasites; water too hot; inflammation; water too acid or alkaline.

**Darkening of color:** *Ichthyosporidium.*

Symptoms of the most common diseases:
1 Bacterial fin rot can affect all fishes but is especially common in Labyrinth Fishes.   2 Pop-eyes and scales that stick out are a sign of ascites caused by *Pseudomonas* bacteria.   3 Hole-in-the-head disease *(Ichthyosporidium)* afflicts mainly Cichlids.   4 White spot *(Ichthyophthirius multifiliis)* is widespread and affects all fishes.
5 *Columnaris* disease can affect all fishes.
6 *Saprolegnia* fungi attack mostly weakened fish.
7 Neon Tetra disease, caused by *Plistophora,* attacks Tetras and similar species more than other fishes.

# Selection and Care of Fishes

**Reddening of skin:** Acidity; ascites (water in the abdomen), also known as Malawi bloat.

**General paling of color:** Lack of oxygen; poisoning; tuberculosis; chill.

**Emaciation:** Tuberculosis and other internal diseases.

**Bloated body:** Ascites, tumors.

**Protruding, inflamed anus:** Enteritis, ascites.

**Bulging eyes:** Ascites; tuberculosis.

**Protruding gills:** Gill parasites; swollen thyroids; lack of oxygen; poisoning.

**Malformations, curvature of the spine:** Genetic abnormality or result of past tuberculosis.

**Fin degeneration:** Tuberculosis.

**Bluish-white dulling of the skin:** Improper acidity of water; parasites, such as *Costia* and *Chilodonella*.

**Sores on the skin:** Ascites; tuberculosis.

**White dots on the skin:** *Ichthyophthirius; Oodinium.*

**Pearl-like or raspberry-like nodules:** Lymphocystis.

There are medications available for most of these diseases. Consult your fish dealer.

It is impossible to keep an aquarium completely free of disease-carrying agents. Even if you take all conceivable precautions, germs will get into the tank through flies, splashing, or normal handling of several tanks. This will do no harm if your fish are healthy and live in a suitable environment. Still, you should have a fish first-aid kit with the most basic medications. After all, fish may get sick on weekends or holidays, when pet stores are closed.

This is what you should have on hand:
• Medication for *Ichthyophthirius* and other protozoan parasites.
• Medication to treat fungus diseases.
• Medication for diseases your particular fish are subject to, such as Neon Tetra disease *(Plistophora)* or Hole-in-the-head disease (caused by *Hexamita*), which often accompanies and aggravates tuberculosis.
• Disinfectant for the tanks and accessories, such as potassium permanganate ($KMnO_4$). You can also prepare a saturated salt solution by adding salt to hot water until the salt no longer dissolves and settles at the bottom.

Important: Most fish medications are brightly colored tablets that look like candies. Keep them away from children.

# *Feeding and Daily Care*

## Feeding Fish

In this day and age commercially available dry food is of such high quality that aquarium fish can live on it exclusively. Also, it is getting more and more difficult to find and catch live food because there is no such thing anymore as a safe, "clean" puddle. Dry food flakes contain not only the necessary nutrients but also vitamins, minerals, and sufficient roughage. They are manufactured in different sizes for different kinds of fish, and there are vegetable flakes for herbivorous fish. Tablets and pellets are also made from the same ingredients as the flakes.

• The first basic rule for feeding fish is: Better too little than too much!

Overfed fish can get sick more easily than slender ones, and overfeeding is bad for the quality of the water as well (see page 12). Feed the fish once or twice a day and only as much as they will eat within five minutes, even if the label says that the food will not cause clouding of the water. It is useful if you have chosen the types of fishes for your community aquarium that will go after their food in a kind of division of labor. The Cyprinodonts and some Pencilfish (e.g., *Nannostomus eques*) feed near the water surface; Corydoras and Headstanders search for food at the bottom; and fish like Neonfish and Angelfish catch what floats around in the water. The last little bits will be consumed by snails, some of which will dig in the ground for food.

With some slow eaters you should not be too strict about the five-minute limit. Headstanders, for example, do not fill their bellies quickly but keep chewing

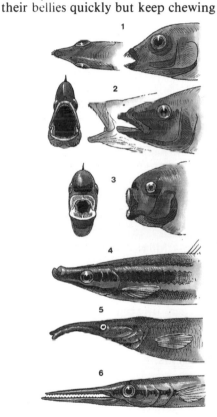

Mouth shapes tell about the eating habits of fish.
1 *Labidochromis* pick and comb small invertebrates from algae.   2 *Haplochromis* hunt fish.
3 *Petrotilapia* scrape algae from stones and rocks.
4 *Anostomus* pick algae from leaves and stones.
5 *Mormyrops* use their trunklike mouths to dig worms and small mollusks and crustaceans out of the mud.   6 *Xenetodon* hunt at the water surface for insects, fish, and frogs.

away all day long. You can estimate how much to feed this way: Take into account that fish food swells up a little in water, and picture how much of this mush it would take to fill the stomachs of all your fish. The amount you come up with will usually be less than what you first thought necessary. It goes without saying that you cannot put food flakes in the tank to be eaten later. Half-grown and fully grown fish are quite able to do without food for a couple of days or even longer. This is not true for very young fish. An aquarium with a lot of leftover dry food is bad for the fish no matter what.

If your fish come rushing to the front glass pane as soon as you approach the tank, this is not necessarily a sign that they are starving, even though it may look like it. It simply means that they have learned that there are often treats when you appear, and they do not want to miss that. If you give in too often and reward their zeal, they will end up with adipose livers and will not live long.

If you do want to give your fish a treat, give them bulky food that fills their stomachs, such as dried daphnia. If you want this food to sink to the bottom fairly quickly, you should first soak it for a little while. That also holds true for other freeze-dried foods, such as mosquito larvae, brine shrimp *(Artemia),* tubifex worms, etc. These are more substantial and make more of a meal than a snack.

• The second basic rule for feeding your fish is:  The very best food is clean live food.

This kind of food keeps fish busy. It contains the correct balance of nutrients as well as both fine and coarse roughage. The contents of the intestines of live feed may, for example, contain vitamins and beneficial bacteria that are particularly valuable for the fish. But this is true only if the live food is fresh. If it is kept alive in storage too long, it is a less healthy food than dry food.

It is easy to introduce pathogenic agents into the aquarium with live foods, and that is why live food should come from water where no fish live. Artificially cultivated live food is safe.

Some of the creatures that serve fish as live food and that you can either catch yourself or buy at the pet store are red, white, or black mosquito larvae, water fleas *(Daphnia),* and tubifex worms.

You can buy *red mosquito larvae* during the winter months. They live on the bottom of streams and lakes and therefore quickly sink to the bottom of an aquarium, where they burrow into the ground and are then available only to certain types of fish, such as Corydoras. They are an excellent food for fish, but they have tough skins. For fry and very small fish they have to be chopped up. This is essential, too, because they can chew their way through the intestine or stomach walls if they are still alive. The chopped larvae are put in a strainer and

# Feeding and Daily Care

rinsed so that the juices will not get mixed into the aquarium water.

You can store a small supply of live larvae outside in cold, shallow water. Larger amounts should be distributed in little heaps in an egg carton, moistened, and put in the refrigerator. They should periodically be rinsed in cold water to keep them from suffocating.

*White mosquito larvae* are not white but transparent. They float horizontally in still water. They make good food for fish but are hard to catch in the icy waters where they live and are expensive to buy. If you have a supply of them, keep them in shallow, icy water or in the refrigerator, as with the red mosquito larvae.

You can catch *black mosquito larvae* during the summer. Larvae and pupae are on the water's surface and breathe air. When disturbed they disappear for a few moments in the water. The pupae are too tough for very small fish. They develop into biting mosquitoes if you let them. Therefore, put no more larvae in your aquarium than will be eaten immediately. Store live larvae in cool, shallow water. The water surface must be large enough that all larvae can stay at the top in order to breathe. In the summer, larvae of biting mosquitoes develop in any body of water no matter how small. If you place bowls of water outside, female mosquitoes will lay eggs in them. In a few days, you will have larvae. After a rainy spell you can catch all the mosquito

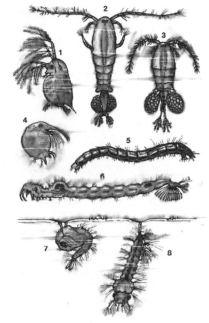

1 Water flea *(Daphnia)*, 2 *Diaptomus* female with eggs, 3 *Cyclops* female with eggs, 4 *Bosmina* crustacean, 5 Red mosquito larva *(Chironomus)*, 6 White mosquito larva *(Corethra)*, 7 Black Mosquito *(Culex)* pupa and 8 larva.
The healthiest food for aquarium fish is biologically raised live food. You can catch the kinds shown above yourself or buy them at the pet store.

larvae you want in flooded meadows, and it pays to place your catch in the freezer.

Water fleas are also summer food. They are small crustaceans of the genera *Daphnia* and *Cyclops,* and they are called "fleas" because of their jumping movements. They live in lakes and ponds, but daphnia in particular are also

Live-bearing Toothed Carps.
Upper left: Wagtail strain of Swordtail *(Xiphophorus helleri);* Upper right: Black Molly strain of ▷
Sphenops Molly *(Poecilia sphenops).*
Middle left: Wild form of *Xiphophorus helleri;* Middle right: Sunset Platy *(Xiphophorus variatus).*
Lower left: Yucatan Sail-Fin Molly *(Poecilia velifera);* Lower right: An ornamental strain of Guppy
*(Poecilia reticulata).*

sold live in pet stores. You will get them packed like fish in plastic bags with water and a supply of oxygen. At home the water fleas that are not used as food right away are kept in plenty of aerated water. If you feed them baker's yeast, they will multiply and be more nutritious for your fish. Mix the yeast with water and feed it to the fleas a drop at a time. The water can get cloudy, but it should never turn milky. As soon as the daphnia have cleared up the water completely, feeding can be resumed, but no sooner. Dissolved yeast spoils quickly. Take only as much as will be used up. You can cut a cake of baker's yeast up into bits and freeze them.

The supply of daphnia may develop into a small daphnia farm practically by itself. Daphnia grow best in containers that hold between 5 and 10 quarts (5 and 10 liters) of water. Light aerating that just keeps the water moving without stirring it up is sufficient. If algae start growing in these breeding containers, all the better. When you are ready to use the daphnia as live food, siphon them off, water and all, into a bucket and then strain them. Fill the breeding container up again with *fresh* water.

In the absence of sufficient food, daphnia produce black "permanent eggs." These can be collected and stored dry. After a vacation of a few weeks, you can start a new farm with them, or you can put them in the tank where the newly hatched larvae will make good eating for

fry. Home growing daphnia like this does not yield a huge crop, but neither does it create dirt or bad odors.

If you do catch enough daphnia or other live food to make freezing worthwhile, carry them home in moistened egg cartons inside a cooler. Freeze the strained live food in sheets 2 millimeters thick. Later, you can break off small pieces for daily use. Because the sheets are so thin, they thaw very quickly and may spoil. When you take them out of the freezer, be careful not to expose any part to heat, such as warm hands. Wear gloves or use potholders when you handle them. Do not place frozen daphnia in the aquarium. Let them thaw for about one minute.

The most common and the cheapest live food is the *tubifex* worm, a red, miniature mud worm that lives in clusters. Tubifex worms are not fattening, and they are a good size for larger fish. They are a good addition to other foods but should not be used as an exclusive diet because they do not seem to be nutritious enough. They also lack roughage. Since they live in mud, tubifex worms will dig themselves into the bottom as soon as they are put into the tank and will leave only their rear ends sticking out for breathing. At any disturbance, the worm instantly contracts, and only the most agile fish will be able to catch it. Burrowing fish like the Corydoras can dig the tubifex out of the bottom gravel, but for all other fish, the

◁ Labyrinth Fishes and Cichlids.
Upper left: Blue Gourami *(Trichogaster trichopterus)*, Cosby strain; Upper right: Flag Cichlid *(Aequidens curviceps)*.
Middle left: Paradise Fish *(Macropodus opercularis);* Middle right: Pearl or Mosaic Gourami *(Trichogaster leeri)*.
Lower left: Siamese Fighting Fish *(Betta splendens);* Lower right: Giant Gourami *(Colisa fasciata)*

tubifex is out of reach there. Tubifex worms use up a lot of oxygen. This deteriorates the water quality, especially at night when plants also consume oxygen.

Important: Feed tubifex at a rate that allows the fish to eat all the worms while they sink to the bottom. Shake up a small cluster of worms with water and distribute over the surface of the water. Do not use food funnels because the less aggressive fish will be pushed away by the stronger ones and will be deprived of their share.

Store tubifex in running water which will clean them at the same time. Tubifex die in stagnant waer. They cannot be spread out or frozen. Before using tubifex as live food, place them in running water for two days so that the muddy intestinal contents are washed away. Do not cut corners. Dirty tubifex are a frequent source of diseases in the aquarium. Washing them is easiest if you have a faucet and drain in the cellar.

### General Advice for Feeding Live Food

Feed fish that have been living exclusively on sterile dry fish food only safe, artificially raised live food at first. As the fish get stronger, their resistance to disease carriers grows, and you can start feeding live food collected in the wild. This is the most well-balanced kind of food, but fish often tolerate it badly if it is introduced too suddenly.

Some aquarium fish (the *Metynnis* species, for example) are strict vegetarians while the Cyprinodonts and others like greens as part of their diet. Generally, lettuce is recommended. But it has been our experience that the health of fish suffers if they are fed commercially raised lettuce that has been treated with chemicals. It is better to feed them plants found in the wild, such as young dandelion greens, chickweed, and other wild plants that people use in salads. Just be sure you gather these plants in places far away from highways and industrial centers. Young spinach leaves are excellent if they have not been sprayed. If your fish are used to lettuce, they may not take to the stronger flavored wild greens right away. Soften the vegetables before feeding by scalding or freezing them first. Anything not eaten within half a day must be removed from the aquarium.

### Caring for Plants

Once a week, or less frequently, you can pick off dead leaves from your plants. There are special plant tongs, but your hands are more accurate and more sensitive. The large leaves of the water lilies *(Nymphaea)* have to be clipped from time to time, or they will shade other plants too much. For the same reason, floating plants have to be thinned occasionally. Duckweed *(Lemna)*, especially, will become a nuisance if some of it is not removed every week or two.

# *Feeding and Daily Care*

This plant is the best water cleaner, and any heavily occupied tank should have a small bunch of it. But it has a tendency to take over if you do not watch out. If the fish stir up a lot of debris in the water, you can shake the plants off from time to time. This is especially advantageous for fine-leafed plants. Fast-growing plants that put out runners can be thinned once in a while so that the growth does not get too dense.

## Care of the Aquarium

We offer below a checklist of those duties you have to perform regularly to make your aquarium into an optimal living environment for your fish.

### Daily Duties
- Feed the fish (see page 59 ff.).
- Observe the fish and check the following points:
Are all the fish coming to the front of the aquarium, or is one hiding in a corner? Are all of them eating? Is their skin clear, or are white dots or discolorations visible? Do they swim upright and easily without rocking, without clamping their fins? Are they darting about nervously? (Water bad or too hot, or electrical insulation damaged.) Are they breathing too rapidly? (Water bad or too hot.)
- Look the plants over:
Are there new shoots, or have leaves dropped off, or are there brown spots? (Bad water, incorrect lighting, not enough $CO_2$. See page 42.) Are there holes in the leaves? (Iron deficiency or too many snails. See pages 42 and 47.)
- Check the water:
Is it clear? Does it smell good, or is it musty or stagnant smelling (see page 13)? Does it smell of dead fish? (Cause for alarm: Find the dead fish.) Are the snails crawling around, or are they lying there motionless? (Warning: Bad water; see page 47.) Is there foam on the water? (Serious warning: Very bad water! See page 13.)
- Check all equipment:
Is everything in working order? Defective motors are usually noisy.

### Weekly Duties
- Groom the plants; thin as needed; remove dead leaves.
- Siphon off debris, not completely but only as needed.
- Clean filters if water flows through them too slowly. Do not be too thorough, or you will disturb the bacterial flora too much (see page 26).
- Clean front panel of the aquarium.
  Remember that all of these activities are upsetting for the fish.

### Frequent Duty
- Change the water. It is better to do this often and in small amounts than to replace a lot of water infrequently (see page 13).

### A Few Helpful Hints for Maintenance Tasks:
- It is easy to check the water for bacteria if you shine a flashlight into the

# *Feeding and Daily Care*

aquarium. If there are too many bacteria, the light will look as though you are shining it into dusty air.

• You can detect floating algae by looking into the aquarium from the side. You can see better this way than if you look down into the water from above.

• If foam is forming at the filter outlet or above the airstone, change about one third of the water right away and again in the course of the next few days. If a foul odor persists despite a change of water, check the bottom material. If it is black and mucky and stinks (hydrogen sulfide), it is high time to dismantle the entire aquarium and to start over with new or thoroughly washed gravel. This is a good time to install a heating cable in the bottom gravel (see page 19) because then no muck will settle, and the aquarium will have to be reconstructed only every two years.

• Be sure to replace at least one third but no more than one half of the water once a month. Use a hose to **siphon** the old water into a bucket. Experienced aquarists prime the hose by mouth without getting water into the mouth. Beginners will probably not be so adept and may prefer to use balloons that are sold for this purpose. When the hose is full of water, the draining will proceed by itself. Discard the old water. Pour fresh water (from the faucet, a rainwater collector, or an ion-exchanger) into a bucket or watering can and then fill the tank carefully. All of this is much easier and

safer if small amounts are exchanged often, about 5 quarts (5 liters) every few days for a 55-gallon (200-liter) tank. The advantages are: The heater does not have to be disconnected because the water level hardly drops at all; the fresh water does not have to be heated beforehand; air does not have to be removed from heavily aerated tap water; fish and plants are only minimally disturbed.

• To siphon off debris, use the hose as described above but place one end carefully at the bottom of the aquarium and use it like a vacuum cleaner to remove the brownish flakes of debris, without picking up the gravel, if possible.

• When you clean the filter, remember that what looks like "dirt" is not all dirt. Some of it consists of working bacteria. As long as water is moving through, there is no reason to clean the filter. But when mud clogs it, it has to be cleaned. Beneficial bacteria are least disturbed if the filter is rinsed with some old aquarium water and not too thoroughly. Some of the bacteria have to stay on the filter. If you have a biological filter (see page 25), you can place a few snails on the filter material. They will eat the surface clean and keep it permeable. The next time you clean the filter, release the snails if they have grown too large, and replace them with smaller ones.

Important: In a half cleaned filter that has not had water running through it for several hours, toxic substances may have

formed. These may destroy the fish when you turn the filter back on. The consequences may not be so drastic, but be sure to wash and rinse a filter that has not been working for a while.
• All maintenance chores are disturbing to the fish. Do them as considerately as you can. Remove water from the surface when you change it. Do chores that involve reaching deep into the water only when absolutely necessary.

## The Aquarium during Vacation Time

When you return from vacation, you would like to find your aquarium exactly as you left it. But are you able to describe exactly what you do when you take care of your aquarium? In the course of daily routine, you have acquired all kinds of little tricks which you perform without thinking but which can be very important. Watch yourself carefully. It is not enough to tell the person who is to look after the fish, "Everything is very simple," as you hand over your aquarium. He or she has to know everything in minute detail. The caretaker should not only do everything correctly, he must also tend the fish and plants the way they are accustomed to being cared for. That is why you should not experiment or introduce new fish shortly before you go away.

This is the way to teach your new caretaker:
• Acquaint him with the fish and their peculiarities, and tell him how many fish there are.
• Tell him what duties have to be performed daily and why.
• Tell him about anything that might go wrong and how to deal with emergencies. Be sure to leave a supply of parts that might have to be replaced (especially fluorescent tubes).
• Demonstrate how you do everything, and watch him imitate you.
• Write down everything he needs to know, including the address and phone number of a dealer whom he can call on for information, the date of your return, and where you can be reached while you are gone.
• Hand him this book so that he can look up things he may need to know.

The following pieces of equipment will help your vacation stand-in with his chores: an automatic heater and an automatic timer for the lights. These are probably already installed in your tank. There are also practical, automatic food dispensers that release small quantities of dry food once or several times a day. If **you are thinking of getting one, buy it at** least two weeks before you go away so that you and your substitute can get to know its quirks. It has to be installed where it is protected from splashing water. If water gets into it and the dry food flakes form lumps, the device will not function. Remember that no automatic gadget is a substitute for a daily check.

# Understanding Fish

Aquarium fish constitute only a small sample of the vast and fascinating world of fishes. In this chapter you will find some information that will help you understand your fish better and interpret their behavior.

## A Brief Introduction to the Study of Fish

Fishes are the oldest vertebrates. The first fishes evolved in the Silurian age about 450 million years ago, and our modern fresh-water species are about 60 million years old. By contrast, anthropoids have been in existence no more than 12 million years, and mankind *(Homo sapiens sapiens)* with its 40,000-year history is a virtual newcomer on this earth.

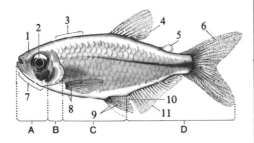

Anatomy of an aquarium fish: A Mouth region, B Gill area, A + B Head, C Body (abdominal cavity extends this far in fish) D Tail region (tail end of body, tail stem, and tail fin), A, B, C, and D together make up the overall length. 1 Nose, 2 Eyes, 3 "Neck" (upper part of body), 4 Dorsal fin, 5 Adipose fin, 6 Tail or caudal fin, 7 Lower jaw, 8 Pectoral find, 9 Ventral fin, 10 Anus, 11 Anal fin.

The earliest vertebrates already possessed all the physical features that still characterize vertebrates, including man: a fully developed skull, a vertebral column, two pairs of extremities, a heart, eyes with lenses, blood corpuscles, and many other features. Even the basic structure of the fish's brain resembles that of ours.

The drawing of a Characin on this page represents a typical fish. Since fishes, in the course of evolution, have spread to every body of water on the earth and have in the process adapted to every conceivable aquatic environment, they have developed the most varied shapes, and even their basic anatomy has undergone all kinds of changes.

The *shape* of a fish tells us a lot about how the fish moves, and even the novice ichthyologist can deduce a fish's way of living from the form of its body. A fish that swims far and fast and has no need for quick turns will be slim and shaped like a submarine. Fish that live among plants swim with greater agility if they are deep-bodied and flat. Fish with a straight back like to be right under the water surface while those with flat bellies tend to hover close to the bottom (see drawing on page 70).

The *fins* serve to propel a fish forward. The main thrust for fast swimming as well as for sudden forward motion is provided by the caudal fin (tail fin) and the muscular tail stalk. Very fast and steady swimmers have forked tail fins

# Understanding Fish

and stiff, stabilizing dorsal fins (see drawing on page 71). Short distances are covered by moving the pectoral fins. These fins are perpetually in motion, even when the fish stands still. That is why pectoral fins are transparent, because visible moving objects are easily detected by predators. A fish's pectoral fins are the equivalent of our arms, and the pelvic fins correspond to our legs. In some species of fish, however, the pectoral fins are located behind the pelvic fins. In Scalares, the two sets of fins are located one directly above the other.

The *skin* of fish, unlike the dry skin of humans, is made up of live cells, including the epidermis. The *scales,* which in no way resemble hair, are completely embedded in the skin and are renewed only if they have been torn out in fights.

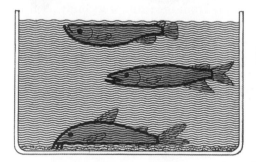

Body shapes are adapted to life styles:
Top: Surface-dwelling fish with undershot mouth and dorsal fin placed way back on body.
Middle: Fish living in the middle strata has normal body shape and normal mouth.
Bottom: Bottom-dwelling fish with flattened belly and overshot mouth.

They grow along with the fish, and it is possible to determine the age of a fish by counting the growth rings on its scales. Fish are exposed to their environment with the entire surface of their bodies. They therefore suffer from head to tail in poor aquarium water.

Fish have *taste buds* not only in their mouths but also on the lips and, if they have any, in the barbels. Some fish even have a few taste buds scattered over the body surface. *Corydoras* and other fish with barbels feel everything they come across on their search for food and know right away whether something is edible and how it tastes.

Just as in man a fish's *sense of smell* is located in the nose. But the nose is not used for breathing because the nostrils are not connected to the oral cavity. The olfactory cells are situated in a short tunnel, the exit of which is right next to the entrance. Motion propels water past the olfactory cells located in this channel, which is reinforced by a small, raised fold in the skin.

The *eyes* of fish are lidless; fish sleep with open eyes.

The organ responsible for *maintaining equilibrium* is the inner ear, which lies inside the skull behind the eyes and is invisible from the outside. This organ is constructed in more or less the same way in all vertebrates. Part of it consists of three miniscule cavities lined with highly sensitive tissue containing otoliths (ear stones). Like the scales, these otoliths

# Understanding Fish

grow with the fish. Gravity pulls them downward, and the sensitive tissue of the cavities tells the fish where the water's surface and the bottom are located. Fish also orient themselves by sight. Any source of light is interpreted as "above." If you shine a light at the aquarium from the side, the inner ear and eye send different messages. For the fish there are now two "aboves," and it will try to align its back with the approximate midpoint (see drawings on page 21). The sense of hearing is also located in the inner ear.

The *swim bladder* enables fish to lie in the water without expenditure of energy. The bladder always has to contain just the right amount of gases. The intake and release of gases is regulated by glands.

The length of a fish's *intestines* depends on its diet. Plant eaters have long intestines and, often, round bellies. Carnivores have shorter intestines and tend to be slimmer. The intestines end in front of the anal fin, which is not necessarily in the rear section of the body.

The *hearts* of fish "are in their throats," far forward in the body and below the gills. The fish heart is the most primitive heart of all vertebrates and consists of only two chambers, the atrium and the ventricle.

The *gills* constitute the breathing apparatus of the fish. From the outside, only the gill covers show, and they constantly open and shut. Fish, like humans, breathe oxygen from the air, but with the

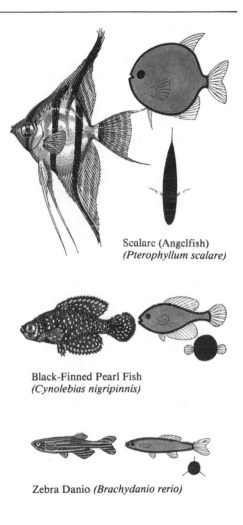

Scalare (Angelfish)
*(Pterophyllum scalare)*

Black-Finned Pearl Fish
*(Cynolebias nigripinnis)*

Zebra Danio *(Brachydanio rerio)*

Fish shapes and motion. Scalares (top) move slowly and quietly among roots and plants; they rarely swim far and fast. Killifishes (middle) often stand motionless in their hiding places but can start up suddenly and cover short distances at lightning speed. Danios (bottom) are fast swimmers with great stamina.

important difference that the air first has to be dissolved in water, much as sugar is dissolved in tea. But only a limited amount of oxygen can be dissolved in water. The water is saturated at about 0.6%. This is very little compared to the 21% oxygen in the air we breathe. It explains why fish have to pump such large amounts of water through their gills in order to get sufficient oxygen. Gills, through relatively small in size, have a very large surface area. If all a fish's gill filaments and lamellae were spread out flat, they would cover the surface of the fish's body several times over. The more active a fish is, the more intensively it has to breathe.

Every cook knows that more sugar or salt dissolves in warm water than in cold. The conditions are just the opposite for air. The colder the water, the more air and, consequently, oxygen it can absorb. At 32°F (0°C) it can take in twice as much as at 86°F (30°C). This means that an icy mountain stream contains more oxygen than a warm, flooded rice paddy. It is no surprise, then, that fishes that live only in cold water in nature do not thrive in a warm aquarium. Their gills and their blood are not designed to extract the small amounts of oxygen contained in such water. In addition, the metabolism of cold-blooded animals accelerates in higher temperatures, and they need even more oxygen. Tropical fish are by nature at ease in warm water, and

they begin to suffer shortness of breath only when the temperature rises above that of their native waters. Fish exhale carbon dioxide and release it into the water through their gills. They can do this only if the water is not saturated with gases. If there is not enough oxygen, a fish starts breathing faster and tries to get air from surface water, which has more oxygen and less carbon dioxide than the water farther down. It "gasps for air," but not literally because the air above the water's surface is practically useless for gill breathing.

The *mouth* is just about the only tool fish have. It is used for catching, chewing, digging, fighting, and sometimes even for carrying eggs or protecting fry. Accordingly, the mouths of fish have become modified into a variety of shapes (see drawing on page 59). There are small mouths made for delicate morsels and wide mouths for bulky food. There are sharp teeth on jaws and tongues for slippery prey, grinding teeth in the pharynx for tough food, and graters on the lips for gnawing off algae. Fish mouths can be classified as normal, overshot, and undershot. A bottom dweller, for example, has an overshot jaw because it gathers its food from the bottom (see drawing on page 70). The shape of the mouth is of interest to an aquarist because it indicates a lot about the type of food the fish can handle.

The *lateral line* could be described as

the fish's sixth sense. This sense organ consists of a canal with sensory cells. It runs along the sides of the body from the rear to the head, where it divides into several branches. The canal is located underneath the scales and communicates with the exterior through a series of pores or little tubes that are visible from the outside as a line of small holes. The lateral line registers even the minutest movement of water. Recent research indicates that many fishes are also able to detect weak electrical currents with their lateral line sense organs. The lateral line tells the fish where other fish are swimming as well as where the echoes of its own fin movements bounce back from. Rivals test their strength by moving the water against their opponents' sides with mighty swats of their tails. This gives the weaker of the two the chance to capitulate before the fight and escape to safety. Fish always respond to sudden vibrations with panic and flight. That is why it is thoughtless and inconsiderate to knock on the glass of the aquarium.

The *coloring and markings* of fish are extremely varied. But there is one recurrent feature: Most fish have silvery bellies. The reason for this is that the silvery belly makes it hard for predators attacking from below to make out their prey against the light water surface. Tropical aquarium fish have both changing and unchanging markings. Some wear the same often spectacular aspect

During the day Pencil Fishes swim among the plants in an upward, slanted position. At night or in a darkened room, they hang just below the water surface in an almost horizontal position, and the markings change. When the day and night cycle is normal, the school will gather twenty minutes before dusk near the water surface, and the change in color will start (internal clock).

day and night. The bright colors insure reliable recognition of other members of the species. Other aquarium fishes change coloring at night. Their "night-gowns" often look quite different from their daytime appearance and make a good camouflage for resting fish. Still other species change their markings within seconds. Like the facial expressions of humans, the markings of the fish are a good indicator of mood. Members of the same species, as well as other fish, understand this language and respond to it. With a little patience you will learn to interpret the meaning of markings and coloring and the movements that accompany changes in them. Then you will be able to observe the family life of fish with greater understanding. This is not only an entertaining pastime; it also facilitates maintaining peace in a community aquarium. When young fish are maturing there are often fights, and it is up to you to recognize the bully and the underdog and separate them before fins start to fly. In a school of young Scalares (Angelfish), for example, the fish start pairing when they are about the size of a quarter. They swim about in twos and develop black spots above their eyes, similar to eyebrows. Young pairs like this try to establish territory in a corner of the aquarium and defend it, even though they are still too small to spawn. Often they stay together for life. The adult Scalare shown on the front cover of this book is defending its spawn and exhibits the characteristic spot above the eye, although the spot is somewhat faded because the fish is frightened of the

A mouth fight between two Cichlids. This most violent form of fighting is common with Cichlids. Both opponents push and pull with all their might.

photographer. The fish is standing at a slight upward angle because this is the position in which it fans fresh water toward the eggs. The spawn is visible on the leaf to the right of its head. Live eggs are light yellow and transparent; the dead ones are white. The latter are removed and eaten. If the young were developed to a later stage, the parent would be swimming horizontally, and the light blue, thread-like pelvic fins would be pointed slightly forward. Twitching of the fins indicates to the young that they are expected to gather around the parent.

## Fish in Their Territory

No matter how fiercely two male Scalares challenge each other at the boundary of a territory during spawning season, a real fight rarely develops. They keep swimming toward each other with extended fins, but they stop short of their adversary and shake themselves. When one of them realizes that he cannot win, he will hang motionless in the water, head tilted upward. At the same time he will emit a kind of creaking noise that is not audible to our ears. He is saying, "I give up; you are stronger." The victor immediately leaves him alone and returns to his brood and his mate. If you have only one pair of breeding Scalares, you can fool the male into thinking that there is a rival by attaching a pocket mirror to the outside of the glass with some tape at

# Understanding Fish

top and bottom. The fish will go into a rage and threaten its mirror image. If you loosen the top tape a little and tilt the mirror slightly, the fish suddenly sees its supposed rival in a conciliatory posture, and it will immediately turn away and go back to its spawn.

Cichlids and Labyrinth fishes are the most violent defenders of territory. If a male has been the sole occupant of an aquarium and you add a female, the male will position himself broadside in front of the female, spread out all his fins as far as possible until the female starts to tremble, and swat with his tail. If you do not understand fish language, you will think that the male is showing off his beauty and welcoming the female joyfully with open fins. The next day, or sometimes as little as twenty minutes later, you will wonder why the female is floating at the top, belly up and without fins. You may be outraged at the viciousness of the fish, but you have simply misread the signals. The spreading of fins, the broadside stance, and the lowering of the bottom of the mouth are all gestures of warning. The male considers the entire tank his territory and will defend it against every other fish. The menacing broadside stance makes the body silhouette look larger and creates the illusion of greater strength.

If you want to introduce other fish into the tank of territorial fish, you usually have to catch and remove the larger ones and place the newcomer in

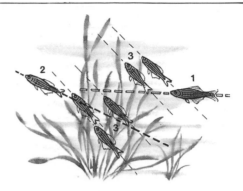

Giant Danios form ranking orders. The highest ranking fish (1) swims in a horizontal position; the lower ranking fish assume a slanting position as soon as a higher ranking one appears. The steeper the slant (2 and 3), the lower the fish's place in the ranking order.

the aquarium first. When it has gotten used to the tank, the others can be brought back. With some very aggressive types of fish, such as the large Cichlids or Tanganyika Mouthbreeders, you may have to rearrange the whole tank to make it look different so that the established fish do not feel quite at home in it. Only if the newcomer is larger than the others can you simply put it into the tank without preliminaries.

## Why Do Some Fish Live in Schools?

The small schools in our aquariums give only a hint of what the huge schools in nature look like. Most fish traveling in schools are small and weak as individuals. The school offers protection. A closely massed school swimming in deep water looks like one large creature from a distance and is not as likely to be attacked. And if an enemy does attack, it is disconcerting to him to be faced with so much look-alike prey. He hardly knows where to start. How does the school react when a predator attacks one of its members? In European minnows it has been observed that an entire school flees as soon as one member as been caught by a pike, and the school will avoid that spot for days afterwards. Specialized cells in the skin give off a substance with a smell when the skin is injured, and this smell spreads quickly, acting like an alarm for the other fish in the school. If a few drops of this substance are put in the water, the minnows display the same panic even though no pike is present. Not all fishes that live in schools produce this "fear" secretion. Among the aquarium fishes that do have it are the Giant Danio *(Danio aequipinnatus),* the Zebra Danio *(Brachydanio rerio),* the Red-Tailed Shark *(Labeo bicolor),* the Rasbora or Harlequin Fish *(Rasbora heteromorpha),* the Chinese Algae-Eater *(Gyrinocheilus aymonieri),* the Black Tetra *(Gymnocorymbus ternetzi),* the Glowlight Tetra *(Hemigrammus erythrozonus),* the Neon Tetra *(Hyphessobrycon innesi),* the Serpae Tetra *(Hyphessobrycon serpae serpae),* and the Black-Bellied Upside-Down Catfish *(Synodontis nigriventris).*

Not every little scratch triggers this fear secretion. But fish of the listed species may be in a perpetual state of fright if one of their kind has been injured somewhat more severely, which can happen when you try to catch one. The injured fish, too, is frightened because it can smell the fear substance but does not know where it comes from. Unfortunately, fish in an aquarium have no way of getting away from the fear-inspiring location. The best thing you can do to relieve their discomfort is to change the water.

The lateral line sense organs help the fish, particularly in the dark or in cloudy water, to discern how far away their closest neighbors in the school are. All the fish keep the same distance from each other, and they never bump into each other. Fishes that swim in bright, clear water — as do many of our aquarium fishes — see each other during the day and do not have to rely exclusively on their lateral line sense organs. They all have easily visible bright colors and immediately recognize members of their species. This knowledge is inborn; it does not have to be acquired. The colors of Neon Fish, Glowlight Tetra, and others also contain guanine, which creates an effect similar to that of aluminum foil. Light striking it is bounced back as by the reflector on a bicycle.

Small fish emit sounds inaudible to our ears, but little is known about the part these sounds play in maintaining the

# Understanding Fish

cohesion of a school. Small Characins constantly send and receive high-frequency sounds. We know that fish are able to distinguish different high-pitched notes played on a recorder and even spoken words. In communicating with each other, some aquarium fishes produce sounds that are loud enough to be heard in the room. It sounds as though the fish were growling, squeaking, or clicking. Upside-down swimming Catfish say a soft "meow" when you catch them and take them from the water. We know very little about the method of sound production in fish. Some crack their joints; some produce sounds with their swim bladders.

Fish do not use just one method to communicate with each other. Usually two or more are used in conjunction: motion and coloration, for example, or sound and scent. Without technical devices we can detect and understand only the movements and the changes in color of fish in an aquarium. But that is quite enough to give us an idea of how our fish are feeling and how to respond to their needs. If you are able to do that you will be rewarded by having fish that are healthy and brightly colored and perhaps even by being successful in your attempts to breed fish.

# Barron's Complete Pet Care Library

*Pet Owner's Manuals*
Bantams
Canaries
Cats
Cockatiels
Dachshunds
Dwarf Rabbits
Feeding and Sheltering
   European Birds
Ferrets
Gerbils
German Shepherds
Goldfish
Guinea Pigs
Hamsters
Long-Haired Cats
Lovebirds
Mice
Mynahs
Nonvenomous Snakes

Parakeets
Parrots
Ponies
Poodles
Rabbits
Snakes
Spaniels
Tropical Fish
Turtles
Zebra Finches

*New Pet Handbooks*
New Cat Handbook
New Aquarium Fish Handbook
New Dog Handbook
New Finch Handbook
New Parakeet Handbook
New Parrot Handbook

*Cat Fancier's Series*
Burmese Cats
Longhair Cats
Siamese Cats

*New Premium Series*
Aquarium Fish Survival Manual
Cat Care Manual
Dog Care Manual
Goldfish and Ornamental Carp
Labyrinth Fish

# Index

# Index

# Index